Annie's Letter
The Story of a Search

Annie's Letter
The Story of a Search

by
Robert Burke

FLYLEAF PRESS

First published in 2004
Flyleaf Press
4 Spencer Villas
Glenageary
Co. Dublin
Ireland.
www.flyleaf.ie
flyleaf@indigo.ie

© 2004 Flyleaf Press

British Library cataloguing in Publication Data available

ISBN 0953997464

Cover design and illustrations:
Cathy Henderson

Layout:
Brian Smith

Acknowledgements

My thanks to the staff and management of the National Archives, Registry of Deeds, Mercer Library, Gilbert Library, Royal College of Physicians, National Library of Ireland, the Representative Church Body Library and the county libraries in Tralee, Castlebar and Wexford for their patience and tolerance.

It would be impossible to list all those who helped in the search, but particular thanks are due to the following each of whom, either wittingly or otherwise, made an important contribution:

Marie Burke, Michael Burke, Russell Charles Burke, Mike Byrne, John Carty, Michael Coady, Bat & Ita Corcoran, Maurine Creagh, John O'Neill Creagh, Gerald Davis, Joe Diskin, Donald Dunn, Terri Garvey, Bill Hogg, Sheila Kerins, Dan King, Prof.J.B.Lyons, Anne Mathews, Olga McConnachie, Dr. Douglas Mellon, Katherine Milburn, Evelyne Miller, Cecily Garvey-Moran, Mary Neill, Seamus O'Boyle, Cathal O Madagain, Mary O'Connor, John O'Connor, Colm O'Daly, Mary O'Doherty, Joan O'Shea, John Sanders, Aileen Sheridan, and Paul Waldron.

Last, but by no means least, very special thanks to Betty McMahon, a best friend and research partner, for her enthusiasm and interest throughout the entire project.

Dedication

In memory of my father Richard Joseph Burke (1898 -1988)

If we do not honour our past
We lose our future.
If we destroy our roots
We cannot grow.

Friedensreich Hundertwasser

(1928-2000)

Contents

Index to Illustrations

One of the outcomes of the author's ten years of research is a significant database of family information. It started as a Burke family tree but has grown gradually to 18,000 persons from all of the families mentioned in this book and many more besides. Readers can access a version of this family database on the Flyleaf Press website at www.flyleaf.ie/burkedatabase.htm. Living persons have been excluded from this version. The database is run on the Brother's Keeper genealogical programme for Windows (version 6). By kind permission of John Steed, the developer of Brother's Keeper, this product can be downloaded from the above page on the Flyleaf website or from www.bkwin.com Full instructions on the database are also provided on this page.

Preface

I hope you will be able to make out my rambling account ... I am afraid if I write much more in this you will never have the patience to wade through.

Most of us have an interest in our roots. For some, particularly in early years, it may be little more than mild curiosity. Others, for whatever reason, want to take their interest further: to persist in finding out about those who contributed to personal appearance, to particular characteristics, to individuality.

There was nothing unusual about my family background. My father was a civil servant, while his father before him worked as a clerk in a hardware business on the north side of Dublin. They were Dubliners, as was my mother. Throughout his life my father enjoyed telling his three children stories about his grandfather and great grandfather, although as time passed, repetition in these stories suggested that his knowledge of his predecessors was somewhat limited. It eventually transpired that all he knew came from one letter in his possession.

The story I have to tell is about how I became involved in searching for the history of our family, and about the surprising revelations that followed. My family tree, the construction of which began in a very modest fashion a few years ago, has grown beyond anything I could have originally imagined.

This could be anyone's story. It is not unusual to assume that we come from a long line of uninteresting ancestors – the idea that this assumption is probably wrong is an intriguing one.

Fig. 1

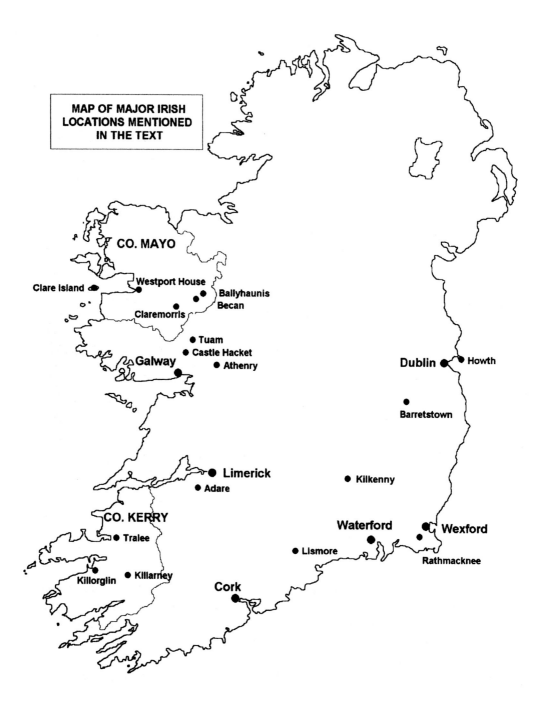

MAP OF MAJOR IRISH
LOCATIONS MENTIONED
IN THE TEXT

CO. MAYO

Clare Island

Westport House

Ballyhaunis
Becan
Claremorris

Tuam
Castle Hacket
Galway
Athenry

Dublin ● Howth

Barretstown

Limerick
Adare

Kilkenny

CO. KERRY

Waterford
Wexford

Tralee

Lismore

Rathmacknee

Killorglin ● Killarney

Cork

[1]
Annie's Letter

There would have been no story to tell if, about a hundred years ago, Annie Goodwin (Fig.2) had not written a letter to her son. The start of this letter is above and the full text is an appendix.

This letter was written by my great grandmother on my father's side, Annie Goodwin. It was addressed to her son, Thomas Burke, who was apparently the amateur family historian of his generation. In the letter Annie tells Tom about his father, Francis Collingwood Burke, his grandfather James Dominick Burke, and about other members of the family. From here on I will refer to this as Annie's letter. It is without doubt the most significant document I possess, as it provided all the facts and clues that eventually led to this trail of startling discoveries.

Although the letter was undated we knew that Annie had been a widow who had remarried to one Colonel Murphy of the US Army and had moved to Indianapolis in 1888. We eventually concluded that the letter must have been written around that year, as her son, my father's Uncle Frank, was in the British army and had been transferred from Carlow in Ireland at about that time.

Tom, to whom the letter was addressed, was an Oblate priest. Tom was sent to Ceylon as chaplain to a British cavalry regiment in the late nineteenth century and on his return was appointed to a parish in Colwyn Bay, North Wales. My father remembers him visiting Ireland in 1909 and mentioning the influence of Tom's grandmother, Louisa Collingwood, on family fortunes. Known to the family as "Uncle Tom", he was reputed to have been a bigoted individual with "no time at all for Protestants". This was very odd, considering that his mother, Annie, was remembered as "a staunch Protestant lady" and presumably his father, his grandfather, and certainly the family of his grandmother Louisa, were all Protestants. Uncle Tom's reputation had preceded him when he came to our house on the only occasion I can remember, not long before his death in 1947. He proved to be a gruff, severe and rather frightening old man and as children we were glad to see the back of him.

From the details of Annie's letter, and from other information collected by my father over the years, my father and I made our first draft of a family tree. (Fig.3) In it I included the names of my father's uncles as he remembered them himself – Thomas, Francis and Russell – and my grandfather, Robert Herbert, along with their dates of birth. This record marked the beginning of what was eventually to become for me an obsession, a never-ending need to learn more and more about my predecessors.

When my father was born, his parents were living in Dublin at no. 3 Sherrard Street, just north of the River Liffey. His father, Robert Herbert, died when my father was a young man, but not before passing on some of his knowledge of our family history.

Robert Herbert's father, Francis Collingwood Burke, an officer in the British army, had secured an appointment in Antigua, in the West Indies, through the influence of his mother, Louisa Jane Collingwood. He took up the position there, but tragically died shortly after arriving, leaving his widow, Annie Goodwin, with four very young children to take care of.

Meanwhile Annie's father had died, and her mother had married again to an Irishman, one Colonel Brennan. Annie's mother and stepfather moved from Annie's birthplace in London to Colonel Brennan's home in Ireland. Annie returned

Fig.2: **Annie Goodwin.**
My great grandmother, unaware of the significance of her letter to son Thomas

from Antigua to their house in Dublin with her children, including my grandfather Robert Herbert, who were brought up in this country. This, we believed at the time, was how we came to be Irish.

From what my father told me, and indeed from Annie's letter, it was clear that we were of a military background, and that my great-great grandmother Louisa Jane Collingwood had been a woman of some social standing. Annie's letter stated that Louisa was the niece of Admiral Collingwood, who had taken over the fleet at Trafalgar after the death of Nelson. My grandfather had always held that it was through the influence of Louisa that Francis Collingwood had secured his position in Antigua.

We had no background whatsoever of James Dominick Burke, Louisa's husband, not even hearsay passed down through the generations (apart from the family heirloom of a toothpick that was reputed to have been his!). My father served in the Royal Navy in World War I and throughout his life he had a great interest in maritime affairs. He used to speculate on how his great grandfather had come to marry into the Collingwood family.

We knew that James Dominick was a surgeon, and it was assumed he had served at the Battle of Trafalgar with Nelson. My father imagined that before the battle Nelson had sent James Dominick, as a trusted officer, to the Collingwood estate in Northumbria in England with a message for Admiral Collingwood, Nelson's second-in-command. In due course Nelson was killed and Admiral Collingwood took over the Fleet. Meanwhile, Surgeon Burke remained in England, having met Admiral Collingwood's niece, Louisa, and married her. This was certainly a good story, but no more than that as it eventually transpired.

In order to move beyond mere speculation, I realised that some genuine research would be needed in order to determine the answers to our questions. The first opportunity to engage in such research came in the form of a working visit paid by myself to Norwich, in England. The location of the birth of my great grandfather, Francis Collingwood Burke, was barely legible in Annie's letter, but to me it looked like 'Lowestoft', which I knew to be fairly close to Norwich.

I decided to find out if a search of parish registers in Lowestoft was a feasible proposition. A number of telephone calls to churches in the town revealed that a certain 'Mr. Hugh Lees' was "an expert on that sort of thing".

One evening during my trip I telephoned Hugh Lees, introduced myself, and asked if there was some way of searching local records. He listened to my story and then, rather abruptly, told me to "hold on". In a matter of a minute or so he was back with details of the baptism of Francis Collingwood Burke and his sister Stephania.

Apparently Hugh Lees had, as a project, analysed every parish register in Lowestoft between the years 1800 and 1820, and had indexed them. This turn of events was truly extraordinary, as it seemed to me at the time most unlikely that I could have come across this information in any other way. It was our first knowledge of my father's grand aunt, Stephania. Annie's letter had referred to her husband's four sisters and one brother, but she had not named them. On the certified copy of the baptism, Francis Collingwood Burke's mother's name was given as 'Louisa Jane' suggesting that she was indeed the 'Louisa Collingwood' so highly spoken of in our family lore, while his baptismal record gave his father's name as 'James Dominique Burke'.

To my father this was an astonishing discovery. Throughout his life he had heard of and read about his grandfather, and yet this was the first time that we had found an actual record of his existence.

Some time later I got the chance to visit Hugh Lees.[1] He was a remarkable man who had been crippled at a very young age and had spent most of his life in a wheel chair. His room was extraordinary – the walls were completely hidden behind books. All of the tables and most of the floor were strewn with papers. Despite the apparent chaos he knew precisely where every book and document was to be found and these he could retrieve with the aid of a long pole-like contraption capable of reaching the highest shelf. It transpired that he was an official of the Suffolk Genealogical Society and he gave me considerable advice and encouragement, suggesting various potential sources of information on my great grandfather, Francis.

The following year I returned to Lowestoft with my father, only to find that Hugh Lees had died. With his passing went a source of help and encouragement, and I sorely regretted not having spent more time with him when I had the chance. My father and I spoke to many people in Lowestoft but found out nothing more of any significance. Where had James Dominick and Louisa Jane been residing before they settled in Lowestoft, and where did they go after they left? The registers at St. Margaret's church in Lowestoft contained no relevant entries other than those for Francis Collingwood Burke and his sister 'Stephania Sarah Saunders Onslow Helen Burke'. This implied that James Dominick and Louisa Jane were not married in Lowestoft, nor did they die there, nor were any of their other children born there.

My father and I met local historians, visited the Maritime museum, the local public library, and the Old Lowestoft & District Society. We learned a great deal about the history of Lowestoft but found no record of a local naval establishment with which James Dominick could have been associated. Local historians told us that maritime records could be examined at Greenwich and at the Public Record Office at Kew, both close to London. We determined to make visits at the earliest possible opportunity.

The search had begun.

[2]
The Story of Annie and Francis

Your father had four sisters and one brother, Russell. Your grandfather Burke died at the age of forty-two leaving six children. Your father often told me about your grandmother marrying for a second time to an officer in the English Army. He was very kind and they got along nicely until one day a favourite horse belonging to the family got very sick. When his stepfather shot the horse your father and his brother were so indignant that they determined to run away and enlist. Your father's love of horses soon made him anxious to join a cavalry Regiment. Through the influence of your grandmother he obtained a transfer to the fifteenth Hussars. He remained in the Fifteenth until he obtained the Staff Appointment in Aldershot in 1860, which is where I met him...

This leg of our story began many years ago at the Public Record Office at Kew, outside London.[2] Our visit there was my first encounter with proper research facilities and I remember well my surprise in finding the benefits of modern technology applied to the business of extracting dusty old documents from the vaults of very large buildings. We were provided with a desk and a computer keyboard and monitor that enabled us to order documents. A bleeper was also provided and this alerted us when our order was ready for collection.

Here we found many old books, reports, records and papers, some of which seemed to have remained untouched by human hand for hundreds of years. After concluding our first visit I recall remarking to my father that we were brushing from our hands dust which had probably lain undisturbed for a couple of centuries. It was of course an experience with which I have since become quite familiar, but I have never forgotten that first occasion.

We discovered a great deal at Kew. To me it was astonishing to find references to 'James D. Burke, Surgeon', and the various ships on which he had served between 1799 and 1808.[3] However, it was disappointing that we found out nothing whatsoever about his personal life. There was no reference to his birth, where he came from, or where he went after his last appointment in 1808. In the many admiralty records and registers of surgeons we found no personal details of the man. He was described as simply 'Dr. Jas. D. Burke'.

While James Dominick remained a remote and enigmatic figure, his son, my great grandfather Francis Collingwood Burke, was rapidly becoming a very real and tangible character in our minds, our visit to the Public Record Office at Kew having no small part to play in that development.

The most significant information we found at Kew on Francis Collingwood Burke was a series of letters from the Governor of the Leeward Islands in the West Indies, the Duke of Newcastle and others. These covered the events that lead up to his appointment as Inspector of Police in Antigua,[4] confirmed the idea that his mother, Louisa Collingwood, had been a woman of considerable influence and, most significantly, the letters dramatically detailed Francis and Annie's fate in the West Indies.

The following extracts from the letters we found show what an extraordinary discovery they were for us.

Antigua
Leeward Islands
20ʰ July 1865

To the Right Honourable
Edward Cardwell M.P.

Sir,
With reference to my dispatch Antigua No. 94 of the 18ᵗʰ instant reporting the lamented death of Mr. Shorediche, I have the honour to inform you that I am not aware of any Gentleman in this or the other islands within my Government qualified to fill the vacant office of Inspector General of Police.

I understand that Quarter Master Sgt. Burke late of the 15ᵗʰ Hussars at present Superintendent of the Military Fire Brigade at South Camp, Aldershot, who was sent out to this island to drill the local Yeomanry Cavalry in 1858, would probably accept the appointment now vacant. As the Sergeant gave the greatest satisfaction when here in the discharge of his duties, I consider it but due to him that I should bring his name and claims under your notice, as from all I have heard he will prove in every way qualified for the Office of Inspector General of Police.

I have the honour to be, Sir,
Your most obedient and humble servant,
Stephen I. Hill
Governor,
Leeward Islands

Under Secretary of State
War Office
29 August 1865

Sir,
I am directed by Mr. Secretary Cardwell to transmit to you the copy of a despatch from the Governor in Chief of the Leeward Islands in which he suggests that the vacant office of Inspector General of Police in Antigua should be offered to Sergeant Burke, Superintendent of the Military Fire Brigade at Aldershot.

I am to convey Mr. Cardwell's request that the appointment should be offered to Sergeant Burke, should there be no objection on the part of the Secretary of State for War or of the Field Marshal R.H. the General Commander in Chief.

I am etc.
J.F.E.

Leeward Islands,
Antigua
8th Dec 1865

Sir,
I have the honour to report the arrival of Sergeant Burke on the 6th instant and his assumption of office of Inspector General of Police in this Island.

I have, Sir, the honour to be
Your obedient servant,
Stephen Hill,
Governor,
Leeward Islands

Annie was sent for once Francis had settled in Antigua. Her children were aged from the four year old twins down to Tom. Husband Francis was already in Antigua when Tom was born in Manchester on the sixth of February, 1866. Annie must have made the long and arduous journey with the infant and the other children from England to the West Indies later in 1866. Soon after her arrival, however, she was left homeless with four very small children to take care of. Her husband died in the first month of 1867, as we learned rather abruptly from the following letter.

Leeward Islands
Antigua
26th January 1867

Governor Hill to
Right Hon. Edward Cardwell, M.P.

My Lord,

I have the honour to report to Your Lordship the death of the Inspector General of Police, Mr. Francis Collingwood Burke who was buried this day.

I have, Sir, the honour to be,
Your obedient servant,
Stephen Hill,
Governor,
Leeward Islands

The dispassionate nature of official correspondence hides the real tragedy of the situation. This was made evident in another letter, found amongst family papers. This letter was addressed to Colonel Brennan who was by then Annie's stepfather, and who was living with her mother in Dublin. It would appear from the letter that Francis Collingwood had asked that his family be sent to Annie's mother in Dublin after his death.

St. Johns
Antigua
27th Jan 1867

Sir,
I trust you will pardon the liberty I am now about to take in addressing you on a most painful subject, viz. the death of my late worthy and highly esteemed friend Mr. Francis C. Burke, which sad event occurred in this City on the 25th instant after a lingering illness – the effects of a diseased heart – leaving a widow and four little ones to mourn his departure.

Mr. Burke, for the space of time he was permitted to remain with us, had deservedly won the respect and esteem of all classes of the community from the highest to the lowest; his friends were many and entertained the highest amount of affection towards him, for in fact to know him was to love him.

It is desirous of carrying out my deceased friend's wishes that his family take passage by the Barque 'Matchless' which will leave this by end of February or first week in March. In the meantime Mrs. Burke and little ones will stop with myself and Aunt who will do the utmost in her power to act a mother's part and will be the means to advising her in all things right and proper. I have forwarded you a newspaper containing editorial remarks relative to the sad occurrence and by which you will find the high favour in which he stood.

With many apologies for trespassing in writing so long an epistle,

I am, Sir,
With great respect,
Yours obediently,
John Shervington

Annie was twenty-six years of age when she made the return sailing across the Atlantic with her four sons to start a new life in Dublin. Although the family had all been born in England, the next generation of children was to be born in Ireland, which explains how my own family came to be Irish. Many years were to pass before Annie wrote to her youngest son, little knowing at the time that her letter would be the inspiration for a revival of interest in family affairs almost one hundred years later.

Our first grandson is Daniel James Collingwood Burke and, at the time of my writing this, he lives with his parents in the U.S. Virgin Islands, where his father is a hotel manager. Daniel was born on St. Thomas, the largest of these islands. To get to the hotel, which is situated on the smaller island of St. John, one has to fly to St. Thomas and then take a boat to the island. St. John must be one of the most beautiful places in the world, and our visits there have been some compensation for having part of our family living abroad.

The island of Antigua is about an hour's flight by small aircraft from St. Thomas. I thought it was truly remarkable that Daniel was born so close to the grave of his third great grandfather. Later I would discover the further significance of Lord Nelson's visit to the Leeward Islands two centuries previously, where he had been married on the island of Nevis.

Fig.3   James Dominick Burke = Louisa Jane Collingwood

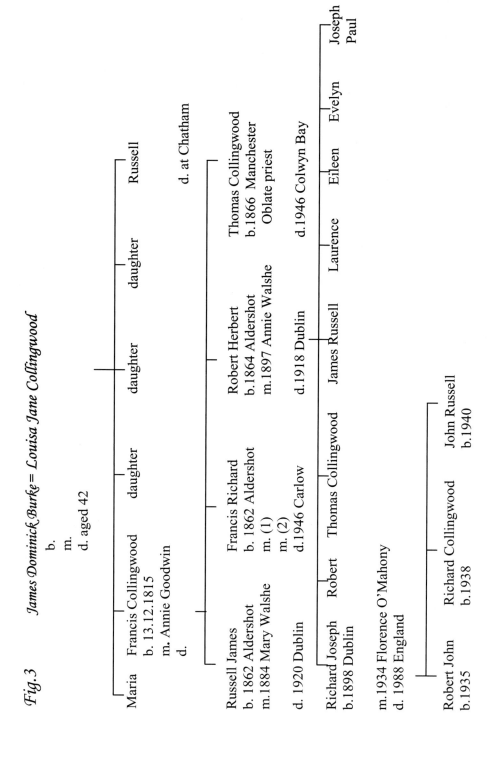

b.
m.
d. aged 42

Maria   Francis Collingwood   daughter   daughter   daughter   Russell
         b. 13.12.1815
         m. Annie Goodwin
         d.   d. at Chatham

Russell James   Francis Richard   Robert Herbert   Thomas Collingwood
b. 1862 Aldershot   b. 1862 Aldershot   b. 1864 Aldershot   b.1866 Manchester
m.1884 Mary Walshe   m. (1)   m.1897 Annie Walshe   Oblate priest
                      m. (2)

d. 1920 Dublin   d.1946 Carlow   Thomas Collingwood   d.1918 Dublin   James Russell   Laurence   Eileen   Evelyn   Joseph
                                                                                                                    Paul
                                                                         d.1946 Colwyn Bay

Richard Joseph   Robert
b.1898 Dublin

m.1934 Florence O'Mahony   Richard Collingwood   John Russell
d. 1988 England   b.1938   b.1940

Robert John
b.1935

On another occasion my wife and I visited Indianapolis on the occasion of the birth of our granddaughter there. It was in Indianapolis that Annie finally settled with her second husband, Colonel Murphy. It came to be, therefore, that our first two grandchildren were born on the other side of the Atlantic Ocean in almost precisely the two locations where Annie had lived a century previously. I did not know at the time that such so-called coincidences were to become a frequent and perplexing feature of the search.

[3]
Uncle Tom's Story

> Your father had a cousin in London, a retired
> paymaster of the Navy, named Walter Burke.
> They had a splendid home. I received a warm
> welcome from him and his wife and daughters
> when we went to London when we were first
> married. He had one daughter who was a nun —
> the other three were very nice girls. He has been
> dead for some years.

My mother died in 1979. I was living in Dublin but for some years after that my father remained outside London where he and my mother had lived for over twenty years. He was in good health and continued to take an interest in the family history. Frequently my work took me from Ireland to the U.K. and occasionally I was able to add a few day's holiday; together we drove to various destinations in search of answers. We rarely discovered anything new, but he did enjoy those trips.

On one particular occasion I suggested that we drive to Colwyn Bay, situated on the north coast of Wales, conveniently close to the car-ferry from Holyhead to Dublin. It was in Colwyn Bay that my father's Uncle Tom's story of our family history had originated. Uncle Tom had claimed that on the wall of a parishioner's house in Colwyn Bay was a family tree which reached as far back as Charlemagne, and that on it he had recognised a link with his own family. This would have been when he returned from Ceylon, presumably in the early years of the last century, after he had received the letter from his mother, Annie.

I remember well our arrival in Colwyn Bay on a Sunday morning, wondering where to start and who to see. I felt rather like the salesman who comes to a town for the very first time with no previous business and no contacts.

We attended eleven o'clock Mass: an inspired start as it turned out. The parish priest was standing at the door when Mass ended, obviously determined to greet each parishioner with a plea for help with the restoration fund, and the last thing he wanted to have to deal with was two strangers enquiring about long-deceased priests of the parish. Indeed it was difficult enough to explain with any brevity why we were there. I began, "my name is Bob Burke, and my father's uncle was a priest here, and he once told us that he had seen a family tree on the wall of a house in Colwyn Bay, probably in the early part of the century..."

To get rid of us, the parish priest suggested that we call to the presbytery where 'Father Cronin might be able to help'. We did this, repeated our story, and to our surprise an elderly Father Cronin remembered working as a young man with Father Tom when both were attached to the parish, shortly before Father Tom's death in 1946. We had a pleasant chat but were told that the only Burkes living in the parish were a young couple recently arrived in town. We were about to leave when Father Cronin recalled that Father Tom used to visit an old lady who lived nearby in a large house. Her name was Blake-Burke, and he felt that she was the sort of person who might have had a family tree. Known as Sammy Blake-Burke, she was dead for more than twenty years. She had left everything to her housekeeper, had never married, and there were no children. This was not what we wanted to hear.

To make matters worse, we were told that the housekeeper had died five years ago. However, Father Cronin told us that her husband was still alive, and was in fact "collecting" at twelve o'clock Mass, and was in the church as we spoke!

So back to the church we went, and there we found Jimmy O'Toole. He told us that his wife never had any belongings of the Blake-Burkes. However, he brought us back to his house and following a trip to his attic produced a photograph of the Blake-Burke family taken around eighteen-eighty or eighteen-ninety. My father and I had little trouble convincing ourselves of a resemblance to our own family! It was a photograph of the parents and five daughters of the Blake-Burke family. One of the daughters was Sammy, but Jimmy did not know which one. He knew that another of the daughters had married and was still living, indeed residing at Booterstown in Dublin. He felt that she might have some information on the family.

Could this have been the family with the Charlemagne tree? Before we left, Jimmy O'Toole recalled that Sammy had connections in London, Australia and, surprisingly, in the Sligo/Mayo area of Ireland. He also told us that Sammy was buried in a family plot at the Franciscan Monastery at Pentasaph, near Holywell, in North Wales.

We travelled to this monastery and examined written records and gravestones but these added little to our knowledge, other than to show that Sammy's mother's name was Annie Blake-Burke – certainly a name from our own family, but far from proof of a connection.

However, a phone call to the Welsh Registry of Deaths revealed that on Sammy's death certificate were the names of her parents. Her father was Walter Blake-Burke, a Major in the army! Could he have been the 'Cousin Walter' of Annie's letter? By now we were sufficiently experienced not to jump to conclusions without seeking proof, but our appetites were sufficiently whetted to ensure that we would do everything in our power to find that proof if it existed.

On my return to Dublin I called on Mrs. Kelly of Booterstown, who told us that one of her sisters had been a nun. By now our information seemed to tally with Annie's letter: 'one daughter was a nun, the others were very nice girls...' We were told that there was indeed a family tree in the possession of the family, held by another Mrs. Kelly, of Emer Street. I called on the second Mrs. Kelly who not only had the document but let me borrow it to show to my father. It was the tree of the Burkes of Ower and did indeed go back to Charlemagne. To our amazement we found ourselves in the possession of the document that Uncle Tom had seen on the wall of a house in Colwyn Bay over half a century previously.

The lines were absolutely fascinating to follow. The tree (which I refer to as the Blake-Burke tree from here on) commences with Pepin, died 768 a.d., through Charlemagne, died 814 a.d., to Harlowen De Burgh and on to William the Conqueror and the subsequent Kings of England. A son of William's, Robert, Earl of Cornwall, produced two De Burgo lines. To one of these belonged Margaret, whose daughter Ellen De Burgo married Robert the Bruce, King of Scotland. To the other line belonged Elizabeth who married the Duke of Clarence, from whom can be traced Edward III, Edward the Black Prince and Richard III. The establishment of the Clanricarde and Ower branches followed. We did discover subsequently that the de Burgo pedigree going back to Charlemagne is well-established, and familiar to those with an interest in Burke genealogy.[5]

At this stage we had built an impressive record of the family, including the maternal lines, and had filled in many details on those who were living in the twentieth century. We did not, however, know how we were connected, if we were connected at all, to the Burkes of Ower and to the lineage of Charlemagne, unless it was through the Walter whose photograph we had found at Colwyn Bay. Neither did we know for certain if we were related to the English family of Admiral Lord Collingwood, as the family lore held, nor did we know the real story of Surgeon James Dominick Burke.

My father died in 1988 without finding answers to any of these questions. He learned nothing more regarding his great grandfather nor did he ever discover if his great grandmother was one of Admiral Collingwood's family. Among his belongings I found my photograph of him, taken standing beside the font at St. Margaret's Church in Lowestoft, where his grandfather was baptised in 1815. Clearly he valued our trips, and together we had indeed achieved something worthwhile.

No advance whatever was made in the period between my father's death and my retirement some four years later. My work was time consuming and necessitated much travelling: this was my excuse for neglecting the project. In retrospect I wonder if the search up to that time was primarily a means of keeping in touch with my father during his ten years as a widower. However, we had discovered a shared interest in family matters, and so when he died I missed his involvement and for a time felt quite isolated.

A few years later, shortly after my own retirement, the whole picture changed.

[4]
Cousins

Your uncle remained with his regiment until he died. He died in Chatham. He was an army apothecary at the time of his death and your aunt received a good pension ...

Throughout my family history search there have been moments that became indelibly imprinted on my memory, the impression of which I doubt will ever fade. The first of these was when Hugh Lees read out over the telephone the names of my great grandfather and his sister, told me the names of their parents and provided a date for their births. It was the first breakthrough. It paled into insignificance compared with the next!

My father was the last of his generation to have had any knowledge of the family history and when he died I realised that the responsibility had been passed on to me. Neither of my brothers nor any of the relatively few cousins I knew of had any interest in family affairs. Quite a responsibility to think that I was now the only living person who knew of James Dominick Burke and Louisa Jane Collingwood, two individuals who had met, married and raised a family almost two hundred years ago. Having traced all of the descendants of their son, Francis Collingwood Burke, I had no idea of what to do next. I must admit that the project had been all but left to one side until one sunny morning, soon after my retirement, when the phone rang in my Dublin home.

With an English accent I was asked if I was Robert Burke. When I confirmed this, the caller suggested that I sit down before he went any further. He then asked if I was a descendant of James Dominick Burke! I can recall the shock of just hearing the words, for to my knowledge there was no person outside my immediate family who could have asked such a question, let alone be aware of the telephone number of the great-great grandson of James Dominick Burke. I did indeed sit down!

The caller was Michael Burke, a jeweller in Hatton Garden, London. He was the great-great grandson of Russell Burke, son of James Dominick and brother of Francis, my great grandfather.

We talked for over an hour. Following the recent death of his father, Michael had developed an interest in his family history and was carrying out his own research in England. He knew of James Dominick, (indeed more than I did, as it transpired) and in an effort to get information on the man, had written to the Royal College of Surgeons in London. They had replied, and remarkably had added that about twenty-five years previously there had been a similar enquiry about the same James Dominick Burke. Thus Michael traced me, and the descendants of James Dominick found each other after almost two centuries.

Michael had a close cousin in England, another Russell, who had inherited various details of the family from his aunt Dorothy, known to the family as Aunt Dot. Possibly the most exhilarating discovery of the entire search was made at this point. Russell had inherited a journal written by James Dominick. The journal described an emigration journey made by James Dominick from Ireland to Liverpool in seventeen ninety-nine!

What this meant, of course, was that James Dominick Burke was Irish, and that we were Irish Burkes! Although I was conscious of the proliferation of Burkes in this country, the prospect of continuing the search on native soil was tantalising. It was incredible to discover this after all those years of having believed we had English roots.

Having emigrated in 1799, James Dominick had made his name in England, married there, and it was sheer chance that brought grandchildren on a sailing ship back from the Caribbean to a house in Dublin. Not only did Michael Burke know that we were Irish, but he believed that we were from a place called Tregunnan, in Mayglass, County Wexford. He had even identified the house, which was called "Mount Pleasant".

Their tree (Fig.4) was constructed from James Dominick (or Dominique) down to the present generation, through James Dominick's son Russell. They had been unaware of any details of Russell's brother Francis and our line. I was already picturing in my mind the impact that all of this would have on our family tree. The excitement was such that both of us were prepared instantly to book the next flight to any convenient location, just to meet and swap notes. Resisting the temptation, we resolved to make arrangements as soon as our cousin Russell was contacted.

Michael sent his family papers and I sent mine. How I wished my father had still been around – he would have been quite astounded to discover another branch of his family stemming from his predecessor of almost two hundred years.

In his biographical details of James Dominick, Michael claimed that James

Fig. 4

James Dominick Burke = Louisa Jane Collingwood

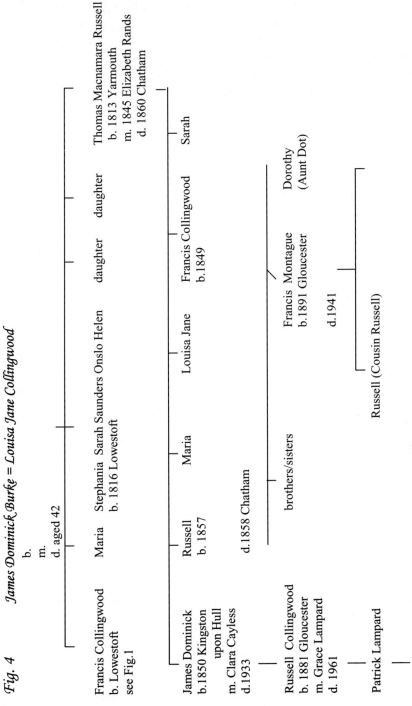

b.
m.
d. aged 42

Thomas Macnamara Russell
b. 1813 Yarmouth
m. 1845 Elizabeth Rands
d. 1860 Chatham

Maria   Stephania Sarah Saunders Onslo Helen   daughter   daughter
b. 1816 Lowestoft

Francis Collingwood
b. Lowestoft
see Fig.1

Russell   Maria   Louisa Jane   Francis Collingwood   Sarah
b.1857   b.1849

d.1858 Chatham

James Dominick
b.1850 Kingston
upon Hull
m. Clara Cayless
d.1933

brothers/sisters

Francis Montague   Dorothy
b.1891 Gloucester   (Aunt Dot)

d.1941

Russell Collingwood
b. 1881 Gloucester
m. Grace Lampard
d. 1961

Russell (Cousin Russell)

Patrick Lampard

Michael (Cousin Michael)

Dominick was born at Mount Pleasant, Co. Wexford in Ireland, circa 1778, studied at Trinity College in 1796, and embarked for Liverpool in England in 1799. Details of the ships he served on coincided with what my father and I had found in the Public Record Office at Kew. Also confirmed was our contention that James Dominick did not take part in the action at Trafalgar. Michael Burke's information suggested that he had married Louisa Collingwood, niece of Lord Collingwood, circa 1810, which agreed with Annie Goodwin's letter. With my father, however, I had established beyond doubt that the Admiral did not have a Collingwood niece. Also it was stated that James Dominick was alive in 1845 when his son Russell was married. Annie's letter, however, had stated that 'Your Grandfather Burke died at the age of 42 leaving six children', which would put the date of his death at around 1822.

James Dominick's journal suggested that he was a student at the Royal College of Surgeons in Dublin,[6] not at Trinity College, and that he had become a ship's doctor, specialising in yellow fever. He was reputed to have left all his assets in trust for the family to his friend Thomas Macnamara. Macnamara, however, absconded with the money. We wondered how much of this was reliable.

When, many years earlier, I had enquired of the Royal College of Surgeons in London if they had any record of James Dominick, they were unable to help me. When Michael asked, some twenty five years later, they found an entry showing that James D. Burke had satisfied the Court of Examiners on 15th May 1800, had paid three guineas, and was described as Surgeon 3rd Rate.

Michael's cousin Russell passed on family notes including considerable detail on the original Russell, son of James Dominick. This traced his army career from his enlistment in 1833 to his discharge in 1855. In 1841 he was bought out for £18 but re-enlisted the same year at Cork. Russell had married, had three sons and three daughters, and appeared to have spent most of his married life in Chatham, in London.

On his discharge from the army Russell was aged forty years, was of fair complexion, was five feet eight inches tall, had grey eyes, and had light brown hair. Somehow this seemed to be such important information, providing as it did a description of an ancestor of that particular generation. Russell had served in Crimea and on his return was declared unfit for further service due to chronic pains and general debility. He survived the battle of Inkermann where British losses were 2,816 men of all ranks. He died in Chatham in 1860.

Russell's full name was, rather incredibly, Thomas Macnamara Russell Burke, presumably named after his father's friend. Clearly Macnamara departed after the christening! Russell's place and date of birth was shown as Yarmouth, September 1815. This was surprising in view of the baptismal certificate from St. Margarets in Lowestoft, showing that his brother was born nine months earlier. Again we wondered about the accuracy of this information.

If we could trace the marriage certificate of James Dominick and Louisa, there was a reasonable chance of discovering their parents' names. What Burke family of county Wexford could afford to send their son to the Royal College of Surgeons? Why did the family think Louisa was a niece of the Admiral? Was it possible that my own family was descended from some established branch of a well-known Irish Burke family?

These were exciting times. Clearly there were contradictions that needed to be checked out, but we now had a comprehensive tree from James Dominick and Louisa down to the present day.

Before the meeting of cousins was arranged, it was agreed that from here on Michael would carry out all the research on his side of the Irish Sea and I would do likewise in Ireland. For the first time in many years the workload would be shared. A plan of action was drawn up which recognised the need for enquiry at the Royal College of Surgeons in Dublin, a trip to Wexford to search in archives for landowners and tenants, a checking of parish registers and eventually graveyard inscriptions.

[5]
Anglo-Irish Efforts

... a niece of Admiral Collingwood ... named Louisa Jane Collingwood ...

The weeks and days leading up to the meeting with my long-lost cousins were filled with anticipation. We met at Milton Keynes, close to the homes of Michael and Russell in the UK.

As it turned out, the meeting was anti-climatic in that no family traits or likeness were immediately identifiable, despite efforts to convince ourselves otherwise. Our interests when it came to the family history were, however, identical.

It felt odd at first to be discussing such an intimate subject with people who until then were complete strangers. Within no time at all we were chatting away as if we had known each other all our lives – indeed the ease with which we became familiar led me to ponder the possibility of a shared gene-pool contributing to a certain likeness of character, even after so many generations.

The three of us spent many hours together, exchanging information, papers, and ideas. We guessed that communication between the families probably ceased when Annie Goodwin came to Ireland with her four young children in 1867, by which time both brothers Francis and Russell had died. Family heirlooms were examined and my toothpick looked rather forlorn beside the journal of James Dominick Burke.

The journal, in appearance rather like a present-day school copybook, was hand-written. James Dominick had commenced writing it in 1799 and the bulk consisted of medical notes. There was however a description of his embarkation at Dublin on 30th May 1799 on the "Ponsonby" packet for Liverpool which was taking French prisoners of war to England. He then took a stagecoach to London, eventually passed his examination and was appointed Surgeon to his first ship. Also included was what appeared to be a draft letter to a lady friend, possibly Louisa Jane.

The story of how it came about that Michael discovered my whereabouts was the highlight of the meeting. In 1955, when Michael was six years old, his parents brought him and his sister on a holiday to Ireland. They visited what his father believed to be the old family home, Mount Pleasant in county Wexford. The gates were locked at the time and they never ventured inside. They found no Burke evidence on tombstones in the local graveyard.

The next occasion when family interest arose for Michael was in the autumn of 1957 when, accompanied by his parents and paternal grandmother, he visited a church and graveyard in the small Kent village of Wouldham, near Rochester. In the graveyard, on the way to the main door of the church, was a large gravestone erected to the memory of Walter Burke, who had been Purser on HMS Victory at the Battle of Trafalgar. Walter was the oldest member of the crew, some sixty years of age, and had been fortunate enough to survive the battle. For some reason Michael's grandmother thought that they were descended from this gentleman.

Thirty years later, Michael visited an antique shop in Piccadilly that specialised in military memorabilia. Sitting in a showcase inside the shop he spotted a miniature coffin, approximately two feet in length. It was perfect in every detail – made of wood, lined in lead, and covered in black paper with fittings painted in gold. On the top of the coffin was an oath, attested by a lawyer and signed over a stamp, claiming that the coffin was one of three made from the timbers of the casket which carried Nelson's body from Chatham to St. Pauls Cathedral, prior to the transfer of the body to it's funeral casket. None other than Walter Burke, the Purser, who made it with his own hands, swore the oath. Michael wanted to believe that Walter was a relative and thought of buying this piece of history, however, the price of one thousand five hundred pounds was enough to deter him, especially as the coffin was not large enough to be used for practical purposes!

Many years later, shortly after the death of his mother, Michael found himself in conversation with an uncle who gave him a piece of parchment. This document was a Warrant of Appointment for a Francis Collingwood to become Commander of HMS Cormorant, dated the twenty-sixth of April 1796. Michael was given the document, together with an unfinished letter apparently from Admiral Lord Cuthbert Collingwood to a Mr. Blackett. This letter was written less than a year before the Admiral's death and appeared to have been in the Burke family for many years.

The Warrant, which Michael had restored and framed, prompted him to investigate this Francis Collingwood to see if he was really related to the Admiral and if there was a connection to the Burke family.

Following contact with the Royal Naval Museum at Portsmouth, the National Maritime Museum at Greenwich, and the Public Record Office at Kew, Michael eventually tracked down details of Francis Collingwood and his son, Francis Edward Collingwood. Deeper research revealed that the Mr. Blackett referred to in the unfinished letter was in fact the Admiral's father-in-law, Lord Mayor of Newcastle upon Tyne. There is a Blackett Street in that city today, right in the centre. Another interesting fact was that Francis Junior had married the daughter of the Reverend Samuel Collis of Fort William in the county of Kerry in 1822. This rather surprising information gave us another Irish connection to be followed up at a later stage.

It was at this point that Michael had his first real breakthrough. His research into Francis Collingwood Junior revealed that he had at least one sister who was by 1828 the widow of Dr. James Dominick Burke and also of the Rev. Hugh Taylor! This was the first mention of James Dominick that Michael had ever found outside of family records. He contacted the Royal College of Surgeons in London, who let him know that he was not alone in his search for the details of the life of James Dominick Burke, and this led to the never-to-be-forgotten phone-call.

Now in possession of the name of Louisa Jane's second husband, further questions were added to our list. Clearly the Rev. Hugh Taylor was not the English officer who shot the horse referred to in Annie's letter, causing Russell and Francis to run away. So the English officer must have been Annie's third husband. Michael's cousin Russell provided us with a collection of letters that went some way toward answering these questions. These showed that Louisa Jane's married name, in 1847, was 'Mulloy'. The first two letters, reproduced here, obviously testify to Louisa Jane's determination in working for her children's success. The first is from Robert Peel, who was then Prime Minister. The second is from Sir John Owen, who was Member of Parliament for Pembroke Dock from July 1841 to 1861.

Whitehall
March 12th 1847

Madam

   I could not ask for the promotion of your sons, except on the ground of their claims for military service. Of their claims I have no means whatever of judging, but the Commander-in-Chief has, and I recommend you therefore to make a communication directly to His Grace to the purport of that which you have addressed to me.

I am, Madam,
Your obedient servant

Robert Peel

Clyffe Hall
28 Nov 1841

Dear Mrs Mulloy

On my return from town I received your letter, which I will present to Lord Hill with the strongest application from myself in favour of its contents. It grieves me to think that your two sons whom I remember so well should be placed in situations so incompatible with their birth and early expectations, and I shall have real satisfaction in doing what I can to improve their prospects. Lady Owen begs her kind compliments and good wishes, and I am

dear Mrs Mulloy

Very sincerely yours

John Owen

Wexford
10th July 1854

I have this instant read your letter of the 5th and I am afraid if I delay writing 'till tomorrow you may not receive a line from me before you embark. I cannot tell you my beloved Russell how grieved I am to hear that you are really going. I kept up my spirits with the hope of your remaining with the Depot, but I suppose that was impossible or I am sure you would have done so. Do write to me my dearest love as often as you can, as it will be the only comfort I shall know while you are away. And be sure to tell me how your wife and children are getting on, particularly my darling Louisa Jane, I feel great interest and affection for them. I am glad poor Frank has returned safe and well. I hope he will soon come to see us and when I hear of your safe return my happiness will know no bounds. I am writing this in a shop where there is a great noise and you must excuse all faults. If you possibly *can, write me a line before you go. God help and protect you my beloved child and send you back to your dear wife and children.*

Your fond and affectionate mother

L. Mulloy

The last letter was written by Louisa Jane to her son Russell, who was obviously about to leave for Crimea. Louisa Jane's third husband had to be a Mr Mulloy, and also had to have been the man who shot the horse.

The value of Michael's work was inestimable. I doubt if I could ever have achieved the same results, working from this country. His efforts were extraordinarily successful.

He found Russell's baptismal record (1813 – not 1815 as previously thought) in Norfolk Archives with his parents names recorded as Dr. James Dominick Burke and Louisa Jane Burke formerly Collingwood. Russell had been born in Yarmouth. Here Michael also found the baptismal record of Russell's sister, Louisa Emma Burke, dated 1810 - thus providing the name of yet another of James Dominick's daughters.

The pace of progress was accelerating. It was as if I was inheriting a rather large jigsaw puzzle, my father and I having found the first few pieces, the picture now building at a startling rate. Of course this was not the conventional jigsaw with 'straight bits' which formed edges, rather there seemed to be no end in sight to the amount of information we could possibly uncover.

From record offices in Haverford West in Wales, cousin Russell obtained a copy of the will of Francis Collingwood Senior. This was all Michael needed to persuade him to travel there to examine the County Archives. There he found the baptismal entry for Francis Edward Collingwood born in 1785 with his father recorded as Francis Collingwood and his mother as Sarah, formerly Richbell. The next discovery was even more exciting - he found an entry for our Louisa Jane Collingwood, born 1787 to the same parents. Her father, Francis, was recorded as having died of "the dropsy" in 1799.

However, one particular stumbling block persisted. No record of the marriage of Louisa Jane and James Dominick could be found, nor was there evidence of any burial notices relating to the Collingwood family.

Not far from Haverford West is Pembroke dockyard where James Dominick was surgeon, according to the biography of Francis Edward Collingwood. At St. Mary's church Michael found the baptismal record of another daughter, Catherine Sophia Burke, born in 1817 - father James Dominick Burke, mother Louisa Jane, formerly Collingwood. Their abode was listed as Golden Hill, now a built-up part of Pembroke. So Catherine was the sixth and last child. We now had the names of all the children, only three of which were named in Annie's letter.

The background to James Dominick's later years was interesting. Until 1816 the Naval Dockyard in the area had always been at Milford Haven and many great sailors had sailed from there, including the likes of Nelson. Even today the largest hotel in Milford Haven is called The Lord Nelson. In 1815 the land-owner who leased the dockyard land to the Crown threatened to increase the rent. When he heard this, the King told the landlord that if he did raise the rent then he, the King, would move the Royal Naval Dockyard elsewhere. The demand for the increased rent was made and so the Yard at Pembroke Dock was established by Royal Decree. One of the three official appointments to the dockyard was of Surgeon, to be directly employed at an annual salary of four hundred pounds. James Dominick Burke was the first to hold this post. Bearing in mind that the average wage at the time was about five shillings per week, James Dominick was a well-paid man.

More was to follow. The Norfolk Archives found the birth and baptismal records of the firstborn to James Dominick and Louisa Jane. This was Maria, referred to in Annie Goodwin's letter. Still, however, there was no record of their parent's marriage.

Meanwhile I was building up a photographic record of churches, gravestones, indeed anything which could be captured on camera as these provided welcome relief from the mass of statistics and written detail accumulated on a venture such as ours.

An important lesson was learned, or rather confirmed, from the recent investigations. By researching the Collingwoods we had come across important Burke information such as the baptismal records. It demonstrated the logic of not confining research to the male line. Realising this, we determined to research the Collingwood pedigree even further – after all, there might be a record somewhere of the marriage into the Burke family. In any case, to find a relationship with the Admiral was a continuing challenge. So we constructed our first non-Burke tree, an outline Collingwood record, setting out what Michael had discovered from his maritime investigations and his trip to Wales (see Fig 5).

Michael now planned to follow up Louisa Jane's marriages to Taylor and Mulloy and also to contact the Collingwood family (my father had attempted this without

Fig. 5   COLLINGWOOD FAMILY

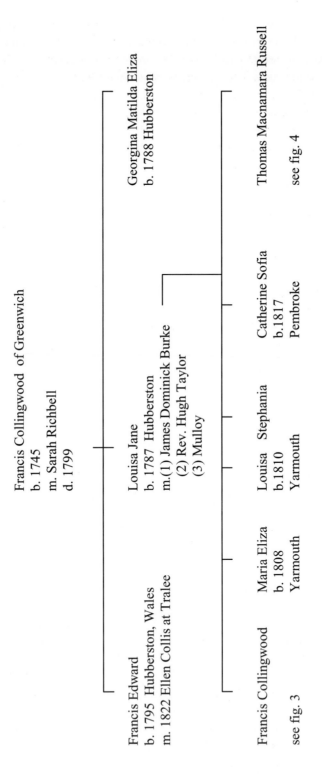

Francis Collingwood of Greenwich
b. 1745
m. Sarah Richbell
d. 1799

Francis Edward
b. 1795 Hubberston, Wales
m. 1822 Ellen Collis at Tralee

Louisa Jane
b. 1787 Hubberston
m.(1) James Dominick Burke
   (2) Rev. Hugh Taylor
   (3) Mulloy

Georgina Matilda Eliza
b. 1788 Hubberston

Thomas Macnamara Russell

see fig. 4

Francis Collingwood

see fig. 3

Maria Eliza
b. 1808
Yarmouth

Louisa   Stephania
b.1810
Yarmouth

Catherine Sofia
b.1817
Pembroke

success some twenty-five years earlier). He would continue checking wherever he felt there might be evidence of the Burke-Collingwood marriage. I decided to make a trip to Wexford to carry out a comprehensive investigation into the Mount Pleasant residence, now that we knew from her letter that Louisa Jane was in Wexford in 1854.

This period was a turning point in my search. The fact that Michael was involved made a great difference. It was less of a lonely pursuit. He had provided an incredible amount of new information on a family history that had taken twenty years to put together. The tree had more than doubled in size, we had branched out into the Collingwoods, and there was no shortage of ideas as to where to look next.

How I wished my father was around to share in the excitement.

[6]
The Journal

...James Dominick Burke ... was a surgeon in the navy.

James Dominick's handwritten notes could be regarded as the most interesting possession to have survived the years. The Royal College of Surgeons in Dublin had expressed an interest in the preservation of the document, particularly because of its medical content. To ensure that this was carried out in a professional manner, the family agreed to hand it over. The College then took responsibility for the exacting copying process needed to ensure that no damage was caused. At the same time I felt compelled to find out what I could about James Dominick's involvement with the medical world.

The Royal College of Surgeons in Ireland (RCSI) was founded in 1784, not long before James Dominick attended. However it was not until 1858 that registration with the Medical Council became compulsory for those wishing to practice medicine in Britain and Ireland. The resources of the Mercer Library of the RCSI include many directories and historical documents. Amongst these are copies of medical directories since 1858 which include details of the qualifications and places of practice of registered doctors. Also included were some obituaries, although biographical details were somewhat limited.

During the course of our discussions I met with the Archivist of the Mercer Library, and I was shown around the inner sanctum. I was generously given a loan of the first edition (1886) of Cameron's History of the Royal College of Surgeons in Ireland. A colleague of mine in earlier days, Professor J. B. Lyons, had written The Irresistible Rise of the R.C.S.I.[6] from which the following relevant extract is taken, describing the medical environment in which James Dominick would have worked.

The familiar barber's pole, striped red and white, is a token of a tradition linking barbers and surgeons, and a reminder of an age when bleeding was a popular therapeutic method. The pole represents the phlebotomist's staff which the unfortunate patient gripped to distend his veins, the red stripe symbolises the fillet placed to obstruct the venous circulation, the white a bandage used when the bleeding was completed. In Dublin the barbers and surgeons were members of the guild of St.Mary Magdalene established by Henry VI in 1446, an association which persisted well into the 18th century, to the disadvantage of the surgeons. Sylvester O'Halloran was born in Caherdavin in 1728 and is credited with the founding of the R.C.S.I. in 1784. In 1789, the new College opened its doors and prospered.

Whereas the journal is a wonderful family heirloom, as a layman I have to admit to some disappointment regarding the content, the bulk of which relates to medical matters. The handwriting is good, not copperplate, but difficult to read due to a rather flowery style. Hence I have had limited success in reproducing some of the non-medical material.

On the inside cover are a variety of James Dominick's 'trial signatures' demonstrating that eighteen year olds have not changed all that much over the years. This is followed by a memorandum of his having attended 'Surgical and Anatomical lectures under Surgeons Hartigan and Dease at the Royal College of Surgeons, Dublin, November 5th 1798.' This was interesting, Dease having been recorded in the College history as dying in June of the same year. What it did mean was that James Dominick had the most distinguished of tutors.

William Hartigan, an early professor of anatomy, became President in 1787. He is remembered as "an amiable oddity; he was dotty on cats and often carried a pair of kittens about with him in the pockets of his greatcoat".

The most distinguished of the founders was William Dease (1752-1798) who held the chair in surgery from 1785 until his death in June 1798. The consensus of opinion was that he took his own life, possibly to escape imprisonment as a United Irishman.

The Irresistible Rise of the R.C.S.I.

The non-medical Journal extracts commence with a description of his emigration:

31 May 1799. Embarked in Dublin on board the Ponsonby packet for Liverpool being appointed by Dr Gray. [On board were] fourteen French prisoners which were to be evicted to the French prison. I arrived at Liverpool on the 1st June and gave the prisoners up. The evening of that day I set out for London in a stage coach and arrived there on the 4th. On the 8th I was examined by the Honbl. Commission for sick and wounded seamen at Commercial house and I passed for surgeon first mate of any rate. [On the] 10th I got my warrant and orders to join His Majesty's Ship the Acteon of 44 guns, [which served] as a Guard Ship in Liverpool. I made my appearance on board on the 13th February 1800. Mr Cudlipp, Surgeon of the Acteon was superseded by Mr I H Dunne. On May 10th [I was given] leave for London for the purpose of passing my examination for Surgeon on the 15th. I passed the College of Surgeons, Lincoln Inns Fields, and was appointed Surgeon first mate of His Majestys Ship Princess Royal 90 guns at Plymouth on the 23rd. I joined the Princess Royal Sept 2nd 1800.

There followed a number of appointments to various ships with details along similar lines. Other entries included a copy of a reference recommending Mr. Jas. D. Burke, a "truly deserving young man", for promotion; a recipe for, and comments on, the "excellent writing ink" that the author had made himself; a prayer used by Prince Eugene, a translation of a sonnet written by Mary Queen of Scots on her passage from France to Scotland, and a poem entitled "Lines Written by a Midshipman".

In addition to these curious entries, there was a whole other dimension to the journal. This consisted of multiple references to the Collingwood family. The first entry was a fascinating account of the ancient Collingwoods, detailing their connection by marriage to King Edward the first, and their apparent inability to avoid wars.

Lord Collingwood's family is of considerable distinction and antiquity in the county of Northumberland, having given to it Knights and Sheriffs during the last three centuries. It was connected by many honourable alliances, of which it is sufficient to mention the marriage in 1627 of his great-great grandfather, Ralph Collingwood, of East Ditchburne, with the niece of Anthony, Earl of Kent, the seventh in descent from Joan Plantagenet, the fair Maid of Kent, who was grand daughter to King Edward the First, and wife, first to the Black Prince and afterwards to Thomas Holland, Earl of Kent. His ancestors are said to have early distinguished themselves in the border wars, and at different times suffered greatly from the indulgence of their martial spirit. In 1585 one of them, Sir Cuthbert Collingwood was, together with the Lord Warden and other knights and nobles, taken prisoner by the Scots. His great grandfather Cuthbert Collingwood of East Ditchburne taking up arms for Charles I lost large estates in the county of Durham. In 1715 George Collingwood of Eslington was sent to death for his attachment to the House of Stuart.

We can only speculate if James Dominick recorded this out of general interest in naval matters or if he had met Louisa Jane and had other ideas. The very next entry, however, strongly suggested the latter.

Dear Madam,

The pleasing hope with which my mind is fortified is too delicate to touch of the soul to be explained, but it is founded on so solid and lasting motives that I am sure it will activate the behaviour of my whole life, for I do not entertain my imagination with these transports only which are raised by beauty. I am not only allured by your person, but am evinced by your life that you are the most amiable of women. Every good being conduct you to that bosom which waits to receive you and protect you from all the cares and vicissitudes of life with an eternal tenderness.

I am ...

One can imagine the difficulties of a young naval surgeon making an approach to a member of one of the most distinguished naval families of the day. Lord Cuthbert Collingwood had taken command of the Fleet at Trafalgar on the death of Nelson, and could have been described as James Dominick's ultimate superior. No wonder James Dominick wanted to ensure that his letter was worthy. It may well have been through Louisa Jane's brother Francis Collingwood, who had himself been distinguished at Trafalgar, that they were introduced.

The bulk of the writings were on medical matters - disappointing to the layman - but to see the two hundred year-old handwriting and signature of a great-great grandfather is a privilege. Now that I had seen his handwriting, I wondered about James Dominick's appearance, what sort of manner he possessed, and what his thoughts and opinions on the personalities and events of his day may have been. He died a young man. Possibly he would have regarded his marriage to Louisa Jane Collingwood to have been his greatest achievement.

[7]
Louisa Jane

... she died quite suddenly when eating her breakfast one morning ...

Dubliners of my generation, particularly those whose parents were Dublin born and bred, are often very familiar with the coastlines of Wicklow and Wexford. There are good reasons for this. Suitable picnic spots were not too far away, the beaches were wonderful, and these acted as reasonable substitutes for any lack of country cousins who might provide summer holidays on distant farms. When our own children were young we had a particularly enjoyable stay in a guesthouse at Rathmacknee in County Wexford.

At that time I was unaware that an Evelyne Miller lived in the Rectory at Rathmacknee. Her house is situated at the end of an avenue and is hidden from the road by large trees. Across the road from the gateway is Rathmacknee cemetery with the ruins of a castle in its grounds. It is a quiet place, a short distance from the Kilmore Quay road and a few miles from Wexford town.

I had made contact with Evelyne on an earlier visit to Wexford immediately following Michael's first phone-call when he informed me of my Wexford origins. Evelyne was a local historian, well respected and referred to frequently by the very active Wexford Family Historical Society.[7] That trip was the commencement of my contact with people, places and genealogical sources of information throughout Ireland. The library in Wexford town was a reminder of the wealth of information available, particularly in those county libraries with local history sections. The experts in Wexford recognized my inexperience in the field of genealogical research and diplomatically suggested that visits to the National Library,[8] the Registry of Deeds,[9] the Royal Irish Academy[10] and the National Archives,[11] all located in Dublin, might be in order. To find out more about the Burke clans I was referred to the many books written on the subject, including branches recorded in various editions of Burke's *Landed Gentry of Ireland*.

On my first trip I had found the Mount Pleasant house and the present owner who lived nearby. The house itself had been unoccupied for about seven years. With the owners, we examined the title deeds which went back to 1828, but which included no reference to the name Burke. Of course, James Dominick's family may only have been tenants. I met many people on this particular visit to county Wexford, and spoke by telephone to Evelyne Miller. She had carried out extensive research into local history back to the seventeenth century and came up with some intelligent questions. She was subsequently to become a great source of encouragement, and made a great contribution to my search. Her 'fantasies', whereby she would speculate upon a possible course of historical events and then go about trying to disprove or support it, were hugely valuable, and a welcome contrast to my own more conservative methods of investigation.

Having researched many families in the area, Evelyne could claim considerable knowledge of Mount Pleasant and the surrounding area. There were in fact two Mount Pleasant houses. The second, known as Little Mount Pleasant, was still occupied and situated across the road from the bigger house. We established that no Burke owner was recorded in the deeds. Around the time of James Dominick, the Harvey family occupied the larger house.

Evelyne became convinced that the Burkes were more likely to have lived in the smaller of the two houses, known as Little Mount Pleasant, and we were taken around that house by it's new owners who were young and enthusiastic enough to want to restore it to it's original condition. They had already removed concrete from floors revealing polished slabs that probably had not seen the light of day for a century at least. We were told that a "Lord Colinwed" had at one time owned the house. Could this have been Collingwood? If so, this would suggest that James Dominick had met his Louisa Jane in Ireland and would also explain why she returned after his death. The hospitality of the local people was much appreciated. They invited us into their homes, fed us on occasions, and went to considerable trouble to help us in our quest. I think they were intrigued by what we had discovered in their locality and were happy to contribute in whatever way they could.

Having returned to Wexford I was becoming more familiar with the area and its history. I revisited the county library and perused parish records at the local Church of Ireland at Killinick, situated close to the Mount Pleasant houses. Was my ancestor Catholic or, better still from the point of view of records, Protestant? Despite all my efforts no relevant Burke entries could be found. I read local histories, studied old newspapers and met a number of people connected with the Wexford Family History Society. In fact I even agreed to join, now that I could claim Wexford ancestry.

I returned to Dublin and visited the National Archives, the National Library and the library of the Representative Church Body,[12] and listed all references I could find to Burkes and Mulloys in the Wexford region. These I recorded diligently but could not see the relevance of any of the details – it emerged later that I had overlooked a very important clue.

Then followed a most remarkable discovery. Evelyne had consulted another publication, 'Memorials of the Dead' by Brian Cantwell,[13] which consisted of an indexed list of gravestone inscriptions from cemeteries in counties Wicklow and Wexford. She sent me a letter containing what could be regarded as the most astounding revelation to date. Having checked for 'Burke' in the index, she found the following:

BURKE, Tombstone with top missing. Catherine Burke who died April 29th 1854 and Mrs Lowisa Jane Mullay who died May 10th 1857 both of Ballyregan in this county

The graveyard in question was Rathmacknee. Evelyne had found the grave of Louisa Jane Collingwood, my great great grandmother, across the road from the entrance to her house! I think she was even more taken aback than I at such an extraordinary discovery.

Back to Wexford without delay! Evelyne and I made our way in heavy rain through the mud, brambles, grass and weeds surrounding the headstones until we came to the grave. It was an unsettling and emotional experience. For so many years, since those bedtime stories as a small child, I had heard the name of Louisa Jane Collingwood. My father had spent many years wondering if she was real, and if she really was a niece of the famous Admiral. He never had an answer, and now my own search had taken me to her grave. I had found her here in county Wexford, her final resting-place.

Considering the family background, how Louisa Jane came to be in this country was puzzling, and where Ballyregan fitted in remained to be seen. Catherine's name was inscribed on the gravestone as "Miss Catherine" and was obviously the unmarried daughter of Louisa Jane. The terribly overgrown grave with its broken headstone was situated in the Protestant section. We noted that Louisa's married name was Mullay, not Mulloy.

On his visit in 1983, Cantwell had noted the poor condition of the church, which was roofless and inaccessible. He went on to describe the graveyard as being in a state of utter neglect with some of the worst dock growth, waist high in some places, which he had ever seen, this almost completely obliterating the memorials.

Lord Walter Fitzgerald reported as far back as 1903 in that year's 'The Journal of the Association for the Preservation of the Memorials of the Dead in Ireland' that the churchyard was 'in a woefully neglected state'.[14]

It seemed appropriate to have the area cleared and the headstone and surrounding brickwork restored. I set about tidying up the area myself, feeling sure that Louisa Jane would have approved! While I was working, I looked over the cemetery wall nearest the ruins of the church. There, on the other side of the wall, was the farmhouse in which we had spent our summer holidays with our children over twenty years before!

[8]
Louisa Jane's Husbands

... your grandmother Burke married three times and was a widow when she died ...

Reflecting on the progress made since Michael's telephone call, it was important to recognise the part which chance had played in our success. Although at the time I was unaware of the Cantwell publications, I suppose I would have come across them eventually even without Evelyne's help. That Louisa Jane Collingwood was buried in Ireland, however, was extraordinary, and that her grave was adjacent to our holiday home in Rathmacknee and across the road from Evelyne's front gates was positively eerie. It felt as if somehow the search had been anticipated and carefully laid clues planted for us to stumble upon, thus slowly but surely revealing the lives and events of so long ago.

Michael's success continued unabated. He visited the Greater London Records Office and there found references to a Hugh Taylor marrying a Louisa Jane Burke at a church in Lambeth, London, in 1823. The record indicated that the marriage took place at Lambeth Palace. Further information from the Church Commissioners revealed that Hugh Taylor had become a priest in 1822 and had died in 1825 at the age of thirty-two years.

Lambeth Palace Library wrote to say that a marriage licence was issued by the Archbishop of Canterbury to a Hugh Taylor and a Louisa Jane Burke, widow, both of St.Marylebone, on the 10th of April 1823. The marriage bond described Hugh Taylor as a gentleman and the bond, which Taylor put up, was two hundred pounds. This would be forfeited should the marriage not take place within the stipulated time. This seemed an extraordinary amount to lodge, especially as we were to find out later that Louisa Jane was not exactly wealthy at the time and as a priest Hugh Taylor was unlikely to have been particularly well-heeled. Why did they bother with a special licence, when the Banns system was active at the time? This was the old system of publicising the details of a forthcoming marriage some months in advance in order to allow for public objections to be made. It would have taken several months, and so a special marriage license could not have sped up the process by more than a few weeks in any event. Could it have been that Louisa Jane had nowhere to live and that a licence would expedite the move into the home of Reverend Taylor? What sort of man was this Hugh Taylor who would take on a widow and six children? By now, Michael had the bit between his teeth, and was determined to find out more.

We obtained copies of the Licence and Marriage Bond and a copy of the marriage entry for our files. The Guildhall Library in London houses an enormous collection of ecclesiastical records and they provided a potted history of Taylor's education and appointments. In addition there was a reference to him being granted a licence "to perform the duty of Charlotte Chapel, Pimlico", of which he may have been the proprietor, by the Vicar of St. Georges, Hanover Square. Michael talked with the present incumbent and, in his own words, learned more history than he ever did at school. For Hugh Taylor to have become the proprietor of Charlotte Chapel indicated that he, contrary to our first impression, was a man of some substance. This would explain his willingness to stand the sum of two hundred pounds for the marriage licence.

The Taylor story was more or less brought full circle when Michael traced Taylor's will at the P.R.O. in Chancery Lane. He and Louisa Jane were living in Pimlico when he died and he left an estate of almost four thousand pounds to Louisa Jane, making her a wealthy lady. Despite the six children this would have made her quite a catch for some gentleman, and indeed one came along, whom we now knew went by the name of Mullay. Louisa Jane's story was rapidly becoming more interesting than that of her first husband!

Tracing the Taylor marriage meant finding another piece in the jigsaw. However the priority continued to be the quest for evidence of Louisa Jane's first marriage to James Dominick, particularly relevant to the search for our Burke ancestors, although we were not having much luck. The National Library of Wales could find no trace of the death certificate or burial record of James Dominick,[15] but they did find Letters of Administration for his estate. He died intestate and the papers included Louisa Jane's declaration, under oath, that the total of his goods, chattels and credits amounted to the sum of two hundred pounds.

By now we were getting a clear enough picture of the circumstances in which Louisa Jane found herself following the death of her husband. The family was living at Golden Hill at the time. This we had learned was a large farmhouse on some acres of land, where the Burkes were tenants. The date of death is not known precisely but the Navy Lists and other sources suggest May was the probable month. James Dominick's successor was appointed on 2nd July 1822. So James Dominick died around May 1822 and by April of the following year Louisa Jane was married again – apparently six children and a mere two hundred pounds were not insurmountable problems!

The Collingwood connection turned up trumps eventually. Michael located a hand-written tree that, as it happened, my father and I had discovered many years previously in the Genealogical Society in London.[16] I ignored it at the time as it was not of the Admiral's line and Louisa Jane was not shown. But now we had the name of her brother, Francis Edward, who was on the tree. This tree gave us the names of all of Louisa Jane's direct predecessors going back to 1575. It also showed that Admiral Lord Collingwood was a first cousin of Louisa Jane's father. So we had found the link. She was a cousin, not a niece.

"The ancient Northumbrian family of Collingwood was seated at Esslington in that county in the early part of the reign of Henry VIII" according to Burkes Peerage. The earliest record I could find of a family member was of John Collingwood of Esslington who was born around 1400 (Fig.6). The family, led by their attachment to the House of Stuart, suffered a great reverse of fortune in 1715.

Sir Cuthbert Collingwood, born in 1575, was once taken prisoner by the Scots – I am not sure what they made of him, but the words of a song by a Scottish minstrel are preserved to the present day:

> *But if ye wald a souldier search*
> *Among them a' wereta'en that might*
> *What name sae wordie, to put in verse*
> *As Collingwood, that courteous knight*

Although the meaning of the verse is not entirely clear, the association of the name of Collingwood with the term 'courteous knight' is unmistakable! Another Collingwood, not shown on the tree, George of Esslington, a Jacobite, having taken part in the rebellion of 1715, was executed.

Descended from Sir Cuthbert Collingwood were two brothers, Cuthbert of Newcastle and Edward, born 1715. Cuthbert of Newcastle was the great grandfather of the Cuthbert who became Admiral and was knighted after the battle of Trafalgar. After his death in 1810, the Admiral's body was brought to England and, after lying in state in the Painted Hall at Greenwich, was buried in the crypt of St. Pauls in London by the side of Nelson. The monument to his memory is in the south transept of the cathedral. His portrait, by Howard, is in the Painted Hall, having been presented by the family.

Fig. 6   *COLLINGWOOD LINEAGE*

John of Esslington
b. c.1400

|

Sir John High Sheriff in 1544
d. 1550

|

Sir Robert High Sheriff in 1551

|

John of Esslington

|

Sir Cuthbert taken prisoner by the Scots in 1575
m. Dorothy Bowles

|

Thomas of Esslington

|

Cuthbert
m. Sarah Frister

|

Ralph of East Ditchburne
b. c.1600
m. Dorothy Grey, niece of the Earl of Kent

Cuthbert   of Ditchburne   Edward of Byker
b. 1628   and Dissington
d.1687
|

Cuthbert
m. Ann Wilkie

Cuthbert of Newcastle upon Tyne   Edward (sailed with Anson)
b.1712   b.1694
d.1775 (father of the Admiral)   d.1779 (grandfather of
                                                Francis Edward – see fig. 5

Admiral Lord Collingwood had only one brother who died unmarried, which confirmed to us that Louisa Jane could not have been his niece. He had a daughter, however, Mary Patience, who married Anthony Denny of Tralee in 1817, thus providing another Tralee connection.

Louisa Jane was a granddaughter of the Admiral's uncle Edward. This Edward was the first Collingwood to be recorded in the naval annals. He was my fourth great grandfather. Born in 1694, he was midshipman with Anson on the first ever round the world sailing made between 1740 and 1744. Afterwards he was patronised by the then Lord Anson and died in 1779 leaving a substantial estate. He lived in an apartment at Greenwich Hospital from about 1737 until his death. Some of his logs have been saved from which it can be seen that he had very good handwriting.[17] Edward was master of the Victory, first-rate flagship of Admiral Sir John Balchen, a short time before her loss in October 1744. I uncovered a chilling description of this disaster.

On 3rd October 1744 the fleet, under Sir John Balchen, then returning home from Gibraltar, encountered a violent storm in which several of the ships were much shattered. On the 4th the Victory separated from her consorts and was never more heard of. It is supposed that she struck upon a ridge of rocks off the Caskets; as from the testimony of the men who attended the lights, and the inhabitants of the island of Alderney, many guns were heard on the nights of the 4th and 5th, but the weather was too tempestuous to hazard boats out to their assistance. In this ship perished near to 1000 men, besides 50 volunteers, sons of the first nobility and gentry in the kingdom.

Naval Commanders

Edward's son, Francis of Greenwich, was Louisa Jane's father. He was a Captain in the Royal Navy and married Sarah, sister of Captain Thomas Richbell, R.N., Chief Magistrate of the Thames Police. Francis had a distinguished career, recorded in the naval annals. We have a list of all his appointments dating from 1757 to 1796 on file. He was a first cousin of Admiral Lord Cuthbert Collingwood.

We had wondered about the names of some of James Dominick's children. Eventually we put two and two together and decided that his first son was named, not after the friend who absconded, but after Admiral Thomas Macnamara Russell, who was Captain of one of the first ships to take on the young James Dominick in 1800. It also transpired that this Admiral's mother was Irish and his paternal grandmother was a Macnamara. Whatever the reason, it was an achievement to establish the origin of "Russell", a name handed down in our family through each generation to the present day.

Equally it followed that James Dominick's second son, Francis Collingwood Burke, was named after Admiral Collingwood. The preoccupation with naval dignitaries did not end there however. James Dominick and Louisa Jane's mysterious daughter, Stephania Sarah Saunders Onslow Helen, of whose life we knew nothing, was almost certainly named after Admiral Sir Richard Onslow and possibly Rear-Admiral Sir George Saunders, both of whom were contemporaries of James Dominick.

A recently published biography of Nelson includes a fascinating description of my illustrious ancestor, the Admiral Cuthbert Collingwood.

Mary Moultray was the young wife of the elderly Commissioner. She was described as pretty, amusing and sympatica. Both Nelson and Collingwood were attracted to her. She seemed to prefer Collingwood who, reserved and diffident, pedantic, even dour on first acquaintance, was a most attractive companion to those whom he grew to know well. She allowed him into her boudoir at Antigua where he helped her curl her hair; and he stood beside her to turn over the sheets of music when she played the piano. He became, in fact, as she put it herself, like "a beloved brother in our house". Tall and strong, his long hair tied behind the coat of his uniform in a queue, he was at this time far more prepossessing than his friend. For Nelson, pale and thin, had had to have his hair shaved off because his scalp itched unbearably when in a malarial sweat. His head was consequently covered by an incongruous and ill-fitting yellow wig.

Nelson - A Personal History [18]

I am never sure of exactly what comes through in the genes, but as a descendant of Collingwood rather than Nelson I am quite happy to quote the above. It was a relief to find that Annie Goodwin's letter was substantially correct in claiming our relationship with the Collingwood family, one of whom I now knew to be my great-great grandmother.

The names of the children of Francis Collingwood and Ellen Collis were included in the Collingwood tree, which gave me more material for my forthcoming visit to Tralee. It was curious that their marriage took place in May 1822 - the month in which James Dominick died. Was it possible that he had died in Ireland while attending the wedding? This might account for the absence of a death certificate or a burial record in Wales.

Francis Edward, Louisa Jane's brother, was to become a leading figure in our search. He served with Nelson and appears in the cockpit in the famous painting of "The Death of Nelson" by Arthur Devis. He is reputed to have killed the French musketeer who fatally wounded Nelson. I discovered various details of his exploits including a most important extract for our particular interest.[19]

He married Ellen, second daughter of the late Rev Samuel Collis, of Fort William in Co. Kerry in May 1822 by whom he had several children. His only surviving sister was the wife of Dr. J. D. Burke, late surgeon of H. M. dockyard at Pembroke, now the widow of the Rev. Hugh Taylor

So this was the family James Dominick Burke had married into. Steeped in naval history, I could only speculate on the circumstances that led to his meeting Louisa Jane. Possibly he knew her brother. Perhaps it was due to his position as surgeon aboard ship. If only we could trace their marriage record. Once again I wished that my father, who had such an interest in maritime matters, could have lived to enjoy the discovery of such a remarkable naval pedigree.

It has constantly been a source of intrigue for me to imagine what characters in my research were like in physical appearance. I have my own picture of Louisa Jane Collingwood. Her cousin the Admiral, on the other hand, can be examined in his portrait, as can her brother Francis Edward. Whenever I think of Louisa Jane Collingwood, I imagine a short, rather plump woman in her fifties: intelligent, domineering and very determined. Is there any justification for this picture? Does the fact that she married three times suggest that she was attractive and I was doing her an injustice? Does her 1824 letter from Wexford to her son indicate a certain warmth of character because she signed herself as "your affectionate mother", or the contrary as she followed this with "L. Mullay"!

Michael's contact with the Collingwood family provided further information of considerable interest. They had unearthed details of Louisa Jane, which stated that she first married James Dominick Burke, secondly Hugh Taylor and thirdly William Mullay. Their record of the family also indicated that William Mullay and Louisa Jane were married at St. George's, Hanover Square on 5th July 1828, and that Mullay died in 1850 and was buried in 'Prospect' cemetery.

Around this time I examined Samuel Lewis's *'Topographical Dictionary of Ireland'*.[20] This is a sort of bible for the genealogist including descriptions of townlands in Ireland around the year 1837. Under Mayglass, County Wexford, I found the following entry:

A parish in the barony of Forth on the road to Bridgetown and Kilmore, containing 1012 inhabitants. The parish comprises about 3250 acres, chiefly under tillage. At a short distance from the village is a large windmill for grinding corn. The seats are Silverspring, the residence of John Nunn, Esq., Thornville of John Lloyd, Esq.,

Mount Pleasant of the Misses Harvey, and Little Mount Pleasant of Mr. Mullay. The parish is in the diocese of Ferns, the rectory forms part of the Union of Gorey and the corps of the deanery of Ferns, and the vicarage, part of the union of Killinick.

Evelyne's guess was correct. Louisa Jane was living with William Mullay, her third husband, in Little Mount Pleasant in 1837.

We were now getting valuable background information, as well as reassurance on matters such as the spelling of the Mullay name. The Collingwood material gave Michael what he needed to find a record of the Mullay marriage.[21] Mullay was so described in the Register of Marriages as a gentleman bachelor, over the age of 21, of Chelsea, London. She signed as Louisa Jane Taylor, a widow. The marriage was by licence, as opposed to the Banns procedure, to show fellow citizens that they had some standing or status in society.

The Collingwood family assumed Prospect cemetery, where Mullay was buried, to be located somewhere in England, although they had never traced it. When Lewis revealed that Mullay was living in Wexford in 1837 it became apparent that the cemetery was more likely to be in Ireland. Returning to Lewis, I found:

At Kiltennel, a parish in the diocese of Ferns, in an ancient burial-ground called "Prospect", are the vaults of the Courtown and Seafield families.

This naturally led to my presuming that Mullay was buried there because of its proximity to Mount Pleasant and, assuming Mullay was indeed an English army officer, its possible military representation ('Courtown and Seafield families'). When we visited the graveyard, however, we found no trace of anyone by the name of Mullay. Neither gravestones nor records could confirm that Mullay was buried there. There were too many unmarked graves.

The answer to the mystery of the identity of Mullay came quite unexpectedly. I was examining newspapers in the National Library when by chance I spotted the following entry in the London Times.

Attempt at Assassination
Hatton Garden Police-office

On Tuesday night last, between the hours of 7 and 8 o'clock, a young man apparently of some respectability, who gave his name as William Howard and his address as No. 36 Red Lion-square, Holborn, the house wherein is held what is called the London Co-operative Society was brought into custody and charged

with the attempted murder and robbery of a gentleman of the name of Mullay. Mr.
Mullay [had] advertised for a mercantile situation and offered a liberal premium
to any person who should succeed in procuring him a permanent and respectable
one.

London Times, 14th Febraury 1828

Could this have been the same Mullay? At first it seemed highly unlikely, but what
I uncovered on the basis of this speculation shows just how valuable speculation
can be. I discovered, in connection with the same case, that his assailant, "William
Howard, alias Joshua Bell, alias Josiah Bell" was ultimately convicted as "guilty to
assault with intent to rob, but not guilty to attempted murder". The victim's name
was William Mullay, who had arrived in London seeking "a mercantile situation".
Apparently, having met at No. 36 Red Lion Square to discuss business matters,
'William Howard' attacked Mullay with a knife and bat.

Another report of the incident included the detail that 'Mullay's father was the
Master of a Bordeaux Trader, from that port to Dublin'.[22] The same report stated
that Mullay's sister was married to a 'Surgical Gentleman of eminence in Dublin,
Mr. Cusack Rooney'. Further details from the London court case confirmed that
Mullay had recently arrived from Dublin and was described as 'a powerful man,
aged about 40'.

Subsequently I found an address for a William Mullay in Stephen Street,[23] Dublin
in 1807. An 1804 marriage record of Cusack Rooney to Miss. Charlotte Mullay,
described as a daughter of James Mullay of Gloucester Street, Dublin,[24] and a
further record in a directory of Merchants and Traders confirming the business
premises of James Mullay and Sons at No. 37 Gloucester Street completed the
picture.

This had to be the William Mullay who married Louisa Jane Collingwood later
that same year of 1828. Under what circumstances could they have met? Mullay's
father was trading between Dublin and Bordeaux. Mullay probably moved to
Wexford having failed to secure employment in London. He had been seeking
"a mercantile appointment" which suggests he may have been involved with his
father in earlier years. All speculation, but intriguing!

Constant reviews took place by telephone between Michael and myself and by
now my approach had changed. I was satisfied to search for additional information
about events already recorded, the sort of detail that helped to elaborate a picture
beyond mere facts and figures. So far it seemed more productive to follow the
lives of the Burke wives than those of their husbands. These were often remarkable
women of tremendous resilience who had brought up their children in the face of

adversity. My interest in Louisa Jane had grown to the extent that any new facts regarding her life were more than welcome. How had she met James Dominick? Where were they married? How did she come to marry Taylor so soon after the death of her first husband? Did she know him or did they meet after James Dominick died?

Because I was now familiar with the workings of the various archives, I took it upon myself to take note of what information was available in the public domain on the Collingwood family in Ireland. The Collingwood research took me back to the 16th century and I came to realise that this was an extremely well known family, with many well-documented branches.

Curiously, in my research on the Burke clans, I noted that while they were plentiful in Galway and Mayo, there did not seem to be any noted examples from the Wexford region. My files were growing at a considerable rate and for the first time I began to experience real difficulty in keeping track of all the information found and recording all the searches made.

In Dublin I met again with the Archivist of the Royal College of Surgeons in Ireland and told her of my search for the origins of James Dominick. We eventually found a record confirming James Dominick's attendance at the R.C.S.I. in Dublin before having emigrated from Ireland. Also was found in the "Army & Navy List" of 1785-1818: "Burke, James, passed 2nd mate 1st rate May 14th 1799. Navy".

The absence of any reference to a Burke family in Wexford, however, was beginning to look suspicious when, out of the blue, Michael came up with an interesting, indeed likely, hypothesis. Could it have been the case that James Dominick was not from Wexford, had never known of Mount Pleasant; he had died long before Louisa Jane and Mullay moved there.

Of course! I wondered why we had not come to this conclusion before now. The reasoning was simple. Assuming Louisa Jane and Mullay moved to Little Mount Pleasant shortly after their marriage in 1828, the children's ages would have ranged from nineteen down to ten. These children would have grown up regarding Little Mount Pleasant as their home. In later life it would be reasonable for them to say they came from Mount Pleasant, and so the mistaken assumption that James Dominick came from Wexford was perpetuated by the family lore down through the years. The more we thought about it, the more logical it seemed.

We had always surmised that James Dominick came from a wealthy family who could afford University fees and now the idea arose that his father might have been a farmer or even a doctor. If James Dominick was attending the College in Dublin, did this suggest there was a better chance that he came from Dublin than from the country? If we were correct, then all the research in Wexford had been in vain.

What to do next to follow up this new and exciting theory was a problem. Records for Dublin circa 1780 to 1800 were available, but without the name of James Dominick's father or any location for his original home it was a daunting prospect indeed. We floated various theories, having at this stage learned the value of speculation and investigation of even the most remote possibility. There was also the question of James Dominick's religion. This is always a most important factor when carrying out research. He may well have been Catholic, but could have converted in order to marry Louisa Jane, to join the Navy, to become a surgeon, or whatever.

All of these questions and speculations seemed to be creating more confusion than clarification. I was still peeved at not having beaten Michael to the James Dominick theory. It now seemed so obvious. The time was right for a breath of fresh air and so I decided to give my mind a rest and head off to Tralee for a few days in the county of Kerry.

Fig.7: ***Russell Burke at Crimea*** (left).
My great granduncle from whom Michael is a direct descendant
- our earliest photograph c.1854.

[9]
From Tralee To Otago

Maria, the eldest daughter promised her dying sister never to leave her children and so she never married but remained with the children even when they moved to Otago, New Zealand . . .

At this stage, the sheer pleasure of these excursions was such that I felt as though I was on a continual holiday. The idea that research was a dull and stuffy pursuit was well and truly buried in my mind by now. The challenge faced upon arriving at some new location with only the most vague notion of what to look for made the work engaging, knowing that at any point a breakthrough could be made.

Homework and some thought are highly recommended before setting off for distant places to carry out local research. Despite having learned this lesson, I repeatedly found that what I needed when I arrived at my destination was back in Dublin. I tried to overcome the problem by taking everything in the car. Then I worried about the car being stolen! Before embarking for Kerry, I tried to do as much preparation as possible.

The object of this trip was to discover what I could of Francis Collingwood and his successors. Because Francis had married a clergyman's daughter, a search in the Representative Church Body library[12] in Dublin for details of the Reverend Samuel Collis of Fort William seemed sensible before I left. There I found that Samuel Collis had been Rector of Ventry in Kerry from 1798 to 1811, and had produced two sons and four daughters. One of these was presumably Ellen, who married our Francis Collingwood. Unfortunately all centralised Ventry parish records were destroyed in the 1922 Public Record Office fire and it was suggested that I contact the present incumbent at Ventry. If any records remained, they would be found locally only.

Overall, the trip was not very successful from the research point of view. Although I met many people and was given several leads for further enquiry, little was known of Fort William. Furthermore, Collingwood was a less than common name in the county. The first stop I made was in Tralee, where the Church of Ireland Rector and his office gave me all the help they could. Fortunately when sending their Parish Register details to the Representative Church Body in Dublin as part of a centralisation programme, they had computerised their files and could therefore provide printouts. I asked them for details of any Collingwoods and awaited results.

In Dingle I was given permission to wander through St. James's Church and the adjoining graveyard off the main street. Not a Collingwood was to be found. I even looked for Burkes, in case James Dominick had died when attending the 1822 wedding, but had no luck. I was told that there was little point in my venturing further to Ventry as the church there was derelict, there was no graveyard, and all local records were held in Dingle. The Ventry records, it was confirmed, were completely destroyed in the 1922 fire.

Eventually, to my relief the following entry was found in the church records at Dingle:

COLLINGWOOD "Mixed" Dingle Register 1781-1828

16th May 1823 Francis Collingwood Lieutenant in the Royal Navy, commanding the Kite Cutter married Ellen Collis, Parish of Dingle

The 1823 date conflicted with 1822 found earlier. Which was the more reliable and was it important?

Apart from this entry, no Collingwood births, marriages or burials appeared to be registered here. However, the Collingwood pedigree uncovered in the Genealogical Society in London showed that four children had been born to Francis and Ellen – Thomas Richbell, Francis Edward, Cuthbert and Samuel.

When I got back to Tralee from the Dingle expedition, the computer records were available from the Church of Ireland and, sure enough, a number of Collingwood baptisms, marriages and deaths between 1853 and 1887 were listed. From these I was able to produce my first draft of an Irish Collingwood family tree. All were direct descendants of my great-great granduncle Francis, and so I had to find more space on the Burke chart on the wall!

The records at Tralee showed that Ellen was buried in 1878 in the New Cemetery in Tralee. Her son Thomas Richbell Collingwood married one Frances in 1853, his occupation being described as Commander R.N. (Royal Navy). They had two daughters, Lucy and Frances, born in 1854 and 1859. Lucy married Charles Curling, Esq., of Adare, Co. Limerick in 1871. Another son of Francis and Ellen, Francis Edward, born in 1825, was buried in the New Cemetery in 1867. I sent all of this information to the Collingwoods in England. I decided to visit the New Cemetery at the next opportunity, although the absence of any records for over a century suggested that the family plot would be difficult to locate.

It was around this time that things began to slow up so far as progress towards finding the origins of James Dominick was concerned. Whereas I was reasonably content to develop the family tree by adding details of the Collingwood family, Michael was more preoccupied with the direct Burke line and was beginning to feel that he had reached a dead-end. He was still sorting out the descendants of Thomas Macnamara Russell, but was getting nowhere with his enquiries at Pembroke for information on James Dominick. No record of James Dominick's death and burial, let alone his marriage, could be found. I was less than hopeful of finding James Dominick's origins somewhere in Dublin. Perhaps for the first time since the joint project started we both began to wonder if we were reaching the end of the line.

With no obvious leads to follow, it became necessary to review our prospects. The most important information probably lay somewhere across the Irish Sea – this was the marriage record of James Dominick and Louisa Jane. We hoped that this would provide the name of James Dominick's father, although this was in no way guaranteed. Presumably Louisa Jane's mother had left Hubberston after the death of her father and Louisa Jane had been married in her new parish – which could have been anywhere.

One of the lessons I had learned from Hugh Lees (see Chapter 1) was that when there is no obvious line to follow, your best bet is to look for a less likely route, and eventually something of importance will turn up. Somewhere in the Collingwood's family records there may have been a note on James Dominick's origins. The Collis connection was also worth pursuing, but even I had to admit that this was a long shot. The Collises had married into the Collingwood family, and not the Burke family.

So we returned to Annie's letter. Three characters that we still had no information on were Bernard, Walter, and Louisa Jane's daughter Maria who had emigrated to New Zealand.

Michael tried to find army records of Major Bernard H. Burke, but without success. I wrote to The Hocken Library of the University of Dunedin in Otago, New Zealand, in an effort to track down some record of Maria, but without the name of her sister's family there was no way of tracing their immigration.

At about this time cousin Russell sent me a photograph of Thomas Macnamara Russell Burke at Crimea (Fig.7). This showed him standing with a horse and included some other soldiers. Feeling that it was about time to put together a representative photographic collection, I browsed through a vast collection of old family snapshots left to me by my father. I had the idea that I should try to assemble three photographs of each individual if possible, taken when young, in middle age and when old. Often a family resemblance can be more easily spotted at a particular age. It was while sorting through these old photographs that I found a small envelope (Fig.8), such as would be used today to enclose a gift card, with the following inscription:

Sept.27th, 74

Miss M. Burke, care of M. Creagh, Esq., Albany Street, Pelichet Bay, Dunedin, Otago, N.Z.

The handwriting looked familiar. Suddenly I realised that this had to have been Maria and her address in New Zealand, along with the name of her brother-in-law! Little did I know that this envelope was to lead eventually to the biggest breakthrough of all in our search for our Burke ancestry.

My only previous New Zealand contact had been the university library in Otago. I wrote again with the recent discovery of the name M. Creagh, and this time I was sent a closely packed four-page reply with a number of enclosures. This was without doubt one of the most exciting postal deliveries I have ever had the good fortune to receive. Included was an extract from the New Zealander newspaper dated September 7th, 1859.

Sept. 5th - Sir George Pollack, 630 tons, Withers, from London and Queenstown. Passengers – Maria E. Burke; John, Michael C.,Randolph, Gertrude and Arthur Creagh...

So we now knew the date of Maria's voyage to the New World and the names of her brother-in-law and his family with whom she sailed, thus keeping her promise to her sister. Interestingly their voyage was not long after the death of her mother, Louisa Jane. I looked again at Annie's letter:

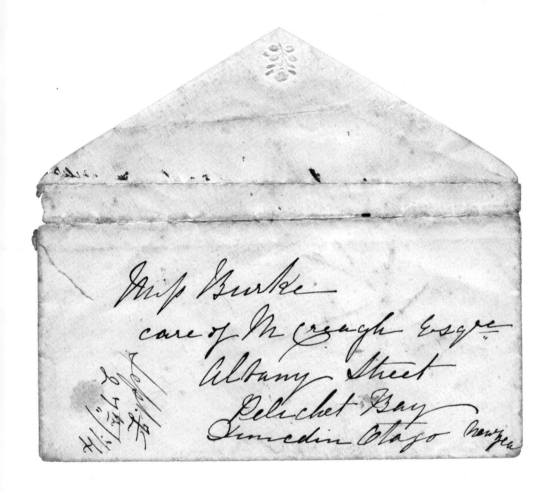

Fig.8: The envelope found amongst photographs in an old shoebox which
provided the most vital clue in the entire search

Your Father had been away for fifteen years when he decided to return to Aldershot. He had hoped to spend a few years with his mother before she died, but the poor fellow was to be disappointed – she died quite suddenly over breakfast one morning before he arrived. Your Aunt Maria had not yet started for New Zealand, and your father and Uncle Russell gave up all claim on their mother's estate and gave it all to Maria. She turned everything to money and, of course, took it with her. I received many letters from her while your father was living but none after his death...

Now I recognised the writing on the envelope – it was Annie's. Presumably Maria and 'M. Creagh' had waited until Louisa Jane's estate was settled before departing. I couldn't help but feel that not surprisingly there was a certain bitterness in Annie's account of Maria's departure with the family money, and of her failure to write after the death of her benefactor.

Among the papers sent by the Hocken Library were copies of marriage records, birth records, tombstone inscriptions, church records, and newspaper clippings, all to do with the Creagh family. I asked myself how this service could be supplied free all the way from New Zealand, while I would be forced to pay for such information from the family history centres in my own country.

Firstly, from burial records we found that 'Michael Creagh', a solicitor, died in 1885.[25] He had been born in Ireland seventy-four years previously where he had married Louisa Emma, nee Burke. So Louisa Emma was the name of the daughter who had died. Maria's full name was Maria Eliza. She died in 1890 and was buried in the Creagh family plot in the Northern Cemetery in Dunedin. She had never married and presumably had never returned to Ireland.

Of the children who had emigrated, Arthur Gethin Creagh was the most prominent. From his death notice we learned that he was born in Dublin in 1850.[26] He would have been a first cousin of my grandfather, Robert Herbert, although almost certainly they were quite unaware of each other's existence. His brother, John, the eldest of the children, must have been Louisa Jane's first grandchild. Arthur Gethin became a solicitor, following in the footsteps of his father, and in 1874 formed the legal firm of Hislop and Creagh, the oldest existing law firm in Oamaru, having been established by Hislop three years previously. In 1885 Arthur Gethin Creagh became Crown Prosecutor in New Zealand. Prior to this he served in the Dunedin Naval Brigade from 1867 to 1875 and became captain of the First Battery in Oamaru. In 1901 he formed the Waitaki Mounted Rifles of which he was captain. A prominent freemason, he died in 1933.

The most intriguing of the newspaper clippings was from 'The Oamaru Mail',

Thursday May 21, 1970. This was a report on the celebrations held for the one-hundredth anniversary of the law firm, Hislop and Creagh. As part of the celebration, the firm published a list of invaluable items which "forged links with the past". These included Arthur Gethin's mahogany desk, the passage ticket of Michael Creagh and family in 1859, Mr. Creagh's diary 1910-1911, the Book of Precedents of John Creagh, brother of Arthur Gethin who practised in Ireland and later in Auckland in 1860. Interestingly, also published were the Genealogical Tables of the Creagh and Collingwood families! (Fig.9).

This wealth of information, which enabled us to produce a Creagh tree, showed that the names "Collingwood" and "Louisa" had been passed down to the present generation, suggesting that the living family may well have been aware of their grandmother Louisa Jane. They might even have had the solution to the mystery that had become James Dominick Burke. Naturally my first instinct was to establish contact with living Creaghs in New Zealand, and again the Hocken Library provided the answer. They managed to trace a great-great granddaughter of Michael Creagh, whose address was in the 1995 Dunedin electoral roll.

It dawned upon me that this genealogical pursuit of mine had now entered a new phase. Having once been "discovered" by my cousin Michael in England, I now had the satisfaction of a similar achievement in finding a hitherto unknown third cousin in New Zealand. It was with a degree of trepidation that I wrote to this lady, but sure enough she knew something of her family history, and was able to send a hand-written Creagh tree that included the following extract:

[Christopher Creagh] born 1486/7 down to Michael born 1811 m. Louisa Emma daughter of James Dominick Burke, surgeon, R.N. She died Monday Jan 5th 1857 and was buried at Mount Jerome Cemetery, Dublin

I arranged for my interest in the Creagh family to be circulated in the 'New Zealand Genealogist' magazine. As a result, I had a response from a descendent of Benjamin Bousefield Creagh who was born at Doneraile in Co. Cork in 1784. This Benjamin Bousefield owned Lanes Brewery in South Main Street, Cork. It became Beamish & Crawford Ltd. in 1905 and still exists as such. My contact was his great-great grandson on the maternal side, who was now living in New Zealand, and was a genealogist to boot! From him I received an incredible amount of information on the Creagh family. All of this prompted me to carry out substantial research here in Ireland and I was eventually able to reconstruct the Creagh line from its origins in Cork to the present day in New Zealand. Later I found that my two New Zealand correspondents were unaware of each other's existence and so, from the other side of the world, I was able to introduce them to one another!

Fig. 9

THE CREAGH FAMILY

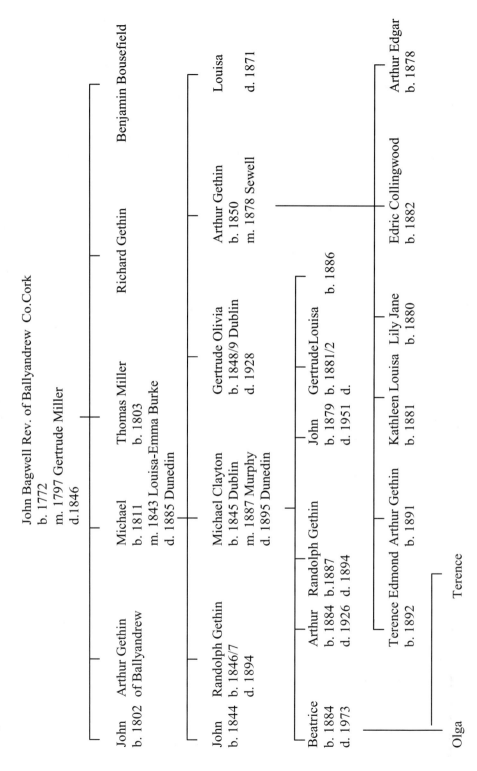

John Bagwell Rev. of Ballyandrew Co.Cork
b. 1772
m. 1797 Gertrude Miller
d.1846

John   Arthur Gethin
b. 1802 of Ballyandrew

Richard Gethin

Thomas Miller
b. 1803
m. 1843 Louisa-Emma Burke
d. 1885 Dunedin

Benjamin Bousefield

Arthur Gethin
b. 1850
m. 1878 Sewell

Louisa

d. 1871

John   Randolph Gethin
b. 1844 b. 1846/7
         d. 1894

Michael
b. 1811
m. 1843 Louisa-Emma Burke
d. 1885 Dunedin

Michael Clayton
b. 1845 Dublin
m. 1887 Murphy
d. 1895 Dunedin

Gertrude Olivia
b. 1848/9 Dublin
d. 1928

John   Gertrude Louisa
b. 1879 b. 1881/2   b. 1886
d. 1951 d.

Edric Collingwood
b. 1882

Arthur Edgar
b. 1878

Beatrice
b. 1884
d. 1973

Arthur   Randolph Gethin
b. 1884 b.1887
         d. 1926 d. 1894

Terence Edmond Arthur Gethin
b. 1892   b. 1891

Kathleen Louisa Lily Jane
b. 1881   b. 1880

Terence

Olga

Christopher Creagh was born about 1486 and became Mayor of Cork. His son, John, was one of those denominated "ancient Irish inhabitants" and as such was expelled from Cork city (Fig.10). He is buried at Clonfert, near Newmarket, Co. Cork. Christopher's great grandson, Michael, was Lord Mayor of Dublin in 1688 and was a Colonel in the service of King James II.

In *Brady's Records of Cork, Cloyne and Ross (1863)* under the entry for Cloyne, Clonfert, it is written that an inscription reading *"Johannes Creagh obiit 8o die martis anno Dom.1768"* is visible on a flat stone near the entrance of the old churchyard. This is the grave of the grandson of William Creagh, who was expelled from Cork in 1644. The descendents of this man still held the lands of Killowend in Clonfert parish when 'Brady's Records' was written. The next entry I found to be even more fascinating.

1774 Oct 16 John Philpot Curran, Esq., and Sarah Creagh, both of this parish were married by licence. The celebrated Curran whose memory is still affectionately remembered was born 24 Aug or Sept 1751 in Newmarket. They had three sons and four daughters, one of whom was Sarah-Gertrude who was baptised at Newmarket on 22nd September 1777; she was "the betrothed of Emmet, wife of Mr. Sturgeon and lies buried in Newmarket. Only a rough stone marks the spot".

When I was a youngster growing up in the old Rathfarnham district of county Dublin, I heard many exciting stories concerning local characters. I recall one describing how Robert Emmett escaped through the window following a raid on "Old Orchard" when he was visiting Sarah Curran. Little did I imagine in those days that there was any family relationship, however remote.

I really did not expect to delve further into this family until I received a family printout from my genealogical correspondent in New Zealand, in response to my request for any further information he might have on the Creagh family. What I received was to me an extraordinary document tracing each generation from Edward III to Michael Creagh, husband of Louisa Emma Burke. Arthur Gethin Creagh is listed in the Royal Descents as being 14th in descent from Edward III. I remembered that Edward III was also included in the Burkes of Clanricarde and Ower tree.

About the time of Charles II, Richard Creagh became Domestic Chaplain to Pope Alexander VII and in recognition of services rendered the Pope granted an augmentation to the Creagh Coat of Arms consisting of a Chevron between Roses. At the request of Michael Creagh, the Crest and Shield were confirmed by Sir Bernard Burke, Ulster King of Arms, in 1854, just a few years before the death of Louisa Emma.

Fig. 10

CREAGH LINEAGE

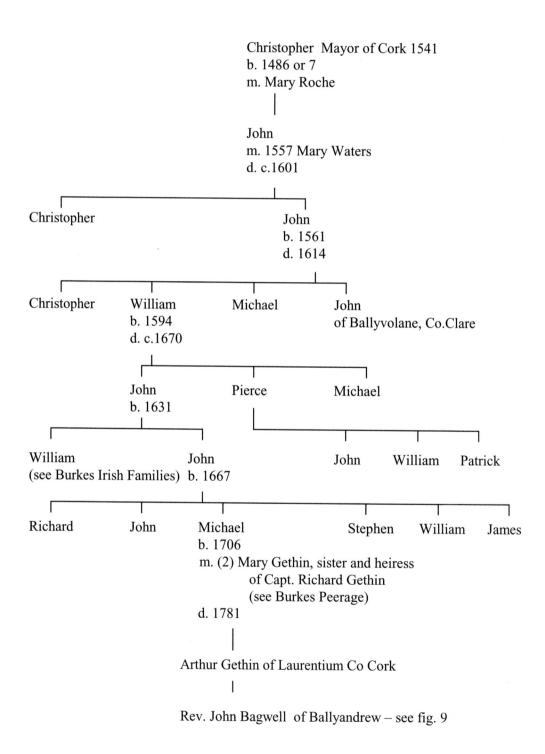

Christopher Mayor of Cork 1541
b. 1486 or 7
m. Mary Roche

John
m. 1557 Mary Waters
d. c.1601

Christopher

John
b. 1561
d. 1614

Christopher   William   Michael   John
                     b. 1594   of Ballyvolane, Co.Clare
                     d. c.1670

John   Pierce   Michael
b. 1631

William   John   John   William   Patrick
(see Burkes Irish Families) b. 1667

Richard   John   Michael   Stephen   William   James
                               b. 1706
                               m. (2) Mary Gethin, sister and heiress
                                       of Capt. Richard Gethin
                                       (see Burkes Peerage)
                               d. 1781

Arthur Gethin of Laurentium Co Cork

Rev. John Bagwell of Ballyandrew – see fig. 9

Richard Creagh had been made Archbishop of Armagh in 1564. At the time Catholics in England and Ireland were attending the 'Established Church' as well as the Catholic Church, in order to stay out of trouble with the authorities. This practice was condemned by the Pope, and apparently the 'zeal of Primate Creagh and others put an end to it'. He was thus made an enemy of the State, who considered his great influence in Ireland to be highly dangerous. He also managed to make himself an enemy of the ruling Irish Prince in Ulster, Shane O'Neill or "Shane the Proud". O'Neill was living with the dowager Countess of Argyll who was the wife of his former captive, O'Donnell, and wanted Creagh to sanction the relationship. Creagh would not do this, and in his rage, O'Neill apparently burned the Cathedral of Armagh. In 1567 Creagh was imprisoned in the Tower of London, and although he escaped once, he was recaptured and died in the Tower after eighteen years of imprisonment. From the Tower, however, he was in touch with the Continent in connection with James Fitzmaurice's endeavours to get support for the War of Religion in the Desmond Revolt. To quote the Creagh family document:

The missions of Wolfe, Creagh and other churchmen have been entirely of a spiritual nature. Circumstances, however, forced upon them the conviction that spiritual conditions demanded physical resistance to the pretensions of the English Government. They were content to counsel both the Holy See and Spain as to the advisability of an invasion.

After much searching I found Louisa Emma's grave – in Mount Jerome cemetery, Harold's Cross in Dublin. A record in the cemetery office described "a granite base with iron railing and a flat limestone tomb". It was granted to "Michael Creagh of 10 Upper Gloucester Street, Dublin on 19th December 1851 for £2.10s.0d. – Louisa 1851; Louisa 1856". I found the grave overgrown with the front part of the railing missing. What I could make out from the headstone read:

Louisa Emma and Louisa, The Wife and Child of Michael Creagh, January 1857

It was an odd feeling to realise that she was buried so close to our home, and that neither my father nor I had been aware even of her existence, let alone the location of her grave.

Now we knew that Louisa Emma (referred to from now on as 'Emma' to avoid confusing her with her mother) had died at the age of forty-seven, only shortly before the death of her mother Louisa Jane, we were able to add considerably to our reconstruction of the events of Louisa Jane's life. Louisa Jane's third marriage to Mullay brought her to the house in Wexford with her six children. It was reasonable to assume that they moved there shortly after their marriage in 1828, although we still did not know why. The children's ages ranged from Maria at nineteen years, down to the youngest, Catherine, who was ten. The boys enlisted in the army in 1833, so possibly they were at boarding school in the meantime. We wondered where.

Mullay died in 1850, presumably while still residing at Little Mount Pleasant, and Louisa Jane and Catherine moved to a nearby house, Ballyregan, sometime after his death. We subsequently found that the daughter Louisa Emma had married Michael Creagh in 1843 and had produced either five or six children before her death in 1857. This was three years after the death of her sister Catherine, but only a few months before her mother died. We were convinced now that this was the Catherine buried with her mother at Rathmacknee. Thomas Macnamara Russell had married in 1845 and had children, so Louisa Jane enjoyed a number of years as a grandmother. It would have been interesting to know how often she saw them and, indeed, if there had been family gatherings – these would have necessitated major journeys between County Wexford, Emma's family in Dublin, Russell Burke in Chatham and Francis Collingwood in Tralee.

Upper Gloucester Street must have been a very select part of Dublin in Creagh's time, running from Marlborough street to Gardiner street Lower in the parish of St. Thomas. In residence there were many lawyers and other professional people. Eventually in the latter part of the century houses in Upper Gloucester Street became tenements and in 1921 the name was changed to Sean MacDermott Street.

In 1835 one Edward Stokes, attorney, had offices at No.3 Upper Gloucester street and at Tralee. Ten years later Michael Creagh was at No.3 with him and by 1855 the firm of Stokes & Creagh, Solicitors, had an office at No.10 and also at Tralee. From the will of Maria Burke, which we found later, we discovered that she was living at No.10 prior to her emigration to New Zealand with Michael Creagh. More pieces of the puzzle fitting together!

The Stokes name was to come up again later leading to questions and more confusion but it did suggest links and relationships between virtually all the families on which I was now concentrating. In an effort to clarify matters I decided to research my Kerry records again.

What I discovered was unexpected. In browsing through Hickson's *Old Kerry Records* I came across a chapter on the lands of Liscahane,[27] Ballybeggan and Ballymullan, which included a reference to a 'Mr. Michael Creagh, a well known Dublin solicitor, who "left his country for his country's good" in or about 1857'.

I wondered what this meant. Leaving for the country's good sounded like a nineteenth century version of "good riddance", yet the expression is shown in parenthesis, presumably having been quoted elsewhere. There was no further reference to Michael Creagh.

Around this time, I was in the National Archives in Dublin searching for the Wills of Collingwoods in the 'Index to Wills and Administrations'.[28] This entailed looking under "A to C" in very large volumes, year by year, in the hope of finding an entry. I was successful in finding one or two wills of descendants of Francis and Ellen, but it was getting late and I decided to leave. The last book had a Collingwood entry which I noted and, as I was putting the book away, as an afterthought I turned to "Burke". Included was an entry for Maria Eliza Burke, the eldest daughter of James Dominick!

Maria Elizabeth BURKE effects £647.3s.8d. 25 Aug 1891. Letters of Administration (with Will annexed) of the personal estate of Maria Eliza Burke formerly of Upper Gloucester Street Dublin but late of Dunedin Otago New Zealand Spinster who died 8 Oct 1890 at latter place were granted at the Principal Registry to Arthur M'Murragh Murphy of 8 Ailesbury Road Co Dublin Esquire and John M'Sheehy 35 Gardiners Place Dublin Solicitor the Attorneys of the Executrix.

It had never occurred to me that Maria would have effects that remained in Ireland after her emigration with the Creaghs to New Zealand. I wondered why my great grandfather and his brother had to give up their inheritance to Maria, who had accompanied Michael Creagh and the children to New Zealand. Was there a financial problem? Why did Maria leave assets here in Ireland? Had Michael and Emma already decided to emigrate or was it a decision resulting from Emma's death? Again many questions, the answers to which might be known in New Zealand. I sensed there was yet another story here.

To complete my construction of the Creagh tree, now that I knew of the Creagh-Burke marriage, I visited the Representative Church Body Library[12] again. Because all of the families were Protestant, and in particular because the Collis and Creagh families included clergymen, this could be a good source of information on their movements, their backgrounds and occasional references to their families. This was something I had established previously when investigating the Reverend Samuel Collis. On this particular occasion I was interested in the Reverend John Bagwell Creagh of Ballyandrew, Emma's father-in-law.

The library contained records of John Bagwell Creagh that I was able to copy for the file, but these were of no great significance. I continued to examine various editions of Burkes Landed Gentry on the shelves without finding any reference to a

Creagh of Ballyandrew. I was about to leave the Library as it was approaching the lunch hour closing, when I was told that there were other volumes in a back room. One of these, very old, without a cover and with pages missing, I recognised as an old edition of *Burkes Landed Gentry of Ireland.*[29] In it was an entry for Creagh of Ballyandrew. What I found was, for me, completely astonishing. Under an entry for the lineage of Christopher Creagh I read the following:

The Reverend John Bagwell Creagh of Ballyandrew had issue 7 sons and 5 daughters:
1. Arthur Gethin, his heir
2. John b.1802
3. Thomas Miller b.1803
4. Michael b. 7/1811 m. 24/5/1843 Louisa Emma, daughter of James Dominick Bourke, of Becan, Co.Mayo, Surgeon R.N. by his wife Louisa Collingwood.

An entry for James Dominick Burke under the lineage of Christopher Creagh, noting his place of origin to be Mayo, in the West of Ireland! Having established the details of two generations of our ancestors' lives in England, I had now discovered that the origin of our line lay in Ireland. The search had commenced many years ago as my father's project, and all along he had the answer to our greatest question buried amongst old photographs which he kept in a shoebox.

[10]
County Mayo

Becan is the residence of J. Bourke Esq. ....

Lewis 1837

My excitement in the Representative Church Body library must have been obvious, because the staff went out to lunch and locked up without asking me to leave. I kept searching and eventually found the following Creagh entry in the 1862 edition of *Burkes Landed Gentry:*

Michael b. July 1811 m. 24/5/1843 Louisa-Emma, daughter of James Dominick Burke of Becan, Co. Mayo, surgeon in the Royal Navy, by his wife Louisa Collingwood, grand-daughter of Edward Collingwood, of the family of Chirton in Northumberland, who accompanied Lord Anson in his celebrated voyage, and was uncle of Cuthbert, Lord Collingwood...

It was difficult at first to accept that we were one of the many Mayo Burkes, while at the same time it was intriguing to think that our search would now turn in a completely new direction – toward Burke clans in the west of Ireland. On the one hand, I was now familiar enough with Dublin's archives to launch into this new line of research with some ease. On the other hand, I was starting all over again.

It was also reassuring to have confirmation of Louisa Jane's connection to the Admiral.

Whereas Michael had always assumed he was of Irish stock, I had subconsciously accepted those English predecessors referred to by my father to have been my ancestors. Now our search had led to us to our mutual origins in a small village in County Mayo.

It was on a Friday that I telephoned Michael with the news, at the same time admitting that I had never heard of Becan. Two days later Michael, walking along the riverbank close to his home in Buckinghamshire, met the mother of a classmate of his daughter. Having engaged in conversation he was unable to resist telling her of the recent discovery of his Irish ancestry. Much to his surprise he learned that her ancestors were also Irish, and that every year she returned to the family farm on holiday. When Michael asked her where this was, she said he would never have heard of it – a very small place in the west of Ireland called Becan! It took Michael several days to get over the shock.

Lewis's 1837 Dictionary,[20] where previously I had found Mullay living in Little Mount Pleasant, had the following entry for Becan or Bekan.[30]

A parish in the barony of Costello, county of Mayo, and province of Connaught, 4 miles from Ballyhaunis containing 5659 inhabitants. It is situated on the road from Claremorris to Frenchpark, and is principally under tillage, with the exception of a few grazing farms. Becan is the residence of J. Bourke, Esq., and Ballenville of J. Crean, Esq. The River Robe has its source within the limits of the parish. It is a rectory and vicarage in the diocese of Tuam, and is part of the union of Kiltullagh; the tithes amount to £127.8.5¼. The R.C. parish is co-extensive with that of the Established Church; the Chapel is a plain thatched building. There are some ruins of the old church with a burial place annexed, which is still used.

There was little doubt in my mind upon reading this that 'J. Bourke' was a descendant of James Dominick, and that we had found the family home. The fact that Burkes Landed Gentry referred to 'James Dominick of Becan' and that my ancestor's family could afford to send him to the Royal College of Surgeons in Dublin was fairly convincing evidence that his was the family holding the seat at Becan.

I decided to assume, for the moment, that James Dominick was a Protestant, bearing in mind that both his wife and children were Church of England. By now I was acquainted with a number of Protestant clergymen in this country and was a regular visitor to the Representative Church Body Library. All were most helpful and, I suspected, anxious to coax me back to the fold, bearing in mind my family history! However, having found Becan on the map, situated roughly between Ballyhaunis, Claremorris and Knock, it became clear that it did not figure prominently in the administration of Church of Ireland parishes. Indeed some of those to whom I spoke seemed unsure of who was responsible for the area.

I was referred to the South Mayo Family Research Centre which is located in Ballinrobe, and it's research covers parts of Mayo including Bekan, Ballyhaunis, Claremorris and Knock. They have built up quite a comprehensive genealogical database of the region from church registers, civil records post 1864, land and property data, gravestone inscriptions and census records. I spoke to them by telephone and it turned out that they were aware of the 'Bourkes of Bekan'. Apparently there was a book available on the history of the parish and although now out of print, they traced a copy to a bookshop in Ballyhaunis.[31] I made an appointment to visit the research centre in Ballinrobe, to discuss whatever information they could uncover on the Becan Bourkes. They told me the Bourkes were Catholics, so it looked like Parish Priests from here on in, and I bade farewell to my newly found Protestant friends in the Church of Ireland.

With difficulty the stranger might find Becan. The only signpost I came across on the route was on the Knock to Ballyhaunis road, and I guessed that this was probably invisible in bad weather. I drove along the narrow roads leading to the village with mixed feelings. I was viewing for the first time a landscape that was familiar to James Dominick when he was growing up as a boy and, in a sense, I felt like I was coming home after two hundred years. On the other hand I had to remind myself that I had felt the same way when looking through the gates of Mount Pleasant in County Wexford, only to realise later that James Dominick had never been anywhere near the place! However, there was now little doubt but that I had found the home of my ancestors. This was a very special day indeed.

My first impression of Becan was tainted by a vague sense of disappointment. I suppose, like the returning Irish-American, I was hoping for a picture-postcard West of Ireland village, whose image could take pride of place in the family album. It would be less than honest to describe Becan in such terms. It was only when I eventually met some of the local inhabitants that Becan began to display a character of its own. It is interesting to realise how it is the people, rather than the landscape, which endow a place with character.

I could hardly believe my luck when one of the oldest residents remembered the Burkes from the turn of the century. The Burkes had lived in Becan House and had been regarded locally as aristocracy. I was told that two elderly ladies, known as Teasy and Bea, were the last of the line. Although no longer well off financially, they had still driven around in a pony and trap. There was also reputed to have been a brother, Charlie, about whom little was known.

The present owner of Becan House showed me around. Her family had added the front of the house in the 1970s. Prior to this the McDonagh family had considerably extended the original house, which they had purchased from the Burkes. The kitchen and outhouses survived the centuries and I guessed that I was looking at the birthplace of those Burkes who flourished throughout the last century. The original home, where James Dominick presumably was born, would have been situated in roughly the same position. There is an orchard and substantial acreage in the grounds of the modern house. It is a large house of five bedrooms in excellent condition. A tree-lined driveway with gardens, and a separate entrance to the farm buildings, gave me the impression that this had been an imposing residence.

I was conscious that in Becan we were reaching farther back into my Burke family history than ever before, and that finding records of the family would not be easy. James Dominick was born around 1780, and had emigrated at the age of eighteen or so. Without any known facts regarding his family we were facing a considerable challenge. It was odd that only now I remembered my father recalling his own father talking about predecessors enjoying holidays in the West of Ireland. I had paid little attention to this at the time, but now it appeared likely to be true, as the Wexford Burkes would have been the first cousins of those Burkes who at the time were still living in Becan.

Following an extensive period of research at the South Mayo Family Research Centre, it was generally agreed that I could assume James Dominick to have been one of the Bekan Burkes. The reference to his name in Burkes Landed Gentry and the R.C.S.I. attendance records were very positive indicators. The staff of the research centre suggested that I make this assumption and then set out to prove it to be correct.

There were various Burke records that I felt may have been of significance. These included the General Register Office death record of John Francis Burke of Bekan, a married man who died on the 20th of March 1886 aged 75 years. The 'informant' of this information was recorded as Charles Burke, son of the deceased. From the returns of the 'Householder Census' of 1901,[32] we learned that Helen L. Burke, age 37, R.C., was living that year in house No. 25, Becan Civil Parish. Birth searches from 1835 to 1859 of Becan Parish resulted in a long list of Burkes from which it was hard to know which entries might have been relevant. There was a record of the marriage of Walter Burke R.C. to Helen Burke R.C., dated the 27th of July 1893, and witnessed by Edward Duffy and Bridget Burke. We also discovered the names Walter Burke and Thomas Burke who may have been from Becan – there was a record of their having received a government grant to grow flax in 1796.[33]

Another outstanding source of information on the area was the book that I located in Ballyhuanis From this book (hereafter referred to as the Becan book), I learned something of the history of the district.

Apparently, in the early 14th century, the area was 'moving into the de Burgo sphere of influence'. This process was interrupted in 1333 however, when William de Burgo, the 3rd Earl of Ulster (the "Brown Earl") was murdered. At that point the local colonists, the Costellos, established themselves as local Lords. In the

16th century, Sir Theobald Dillon was granted lands by the Costellos. Dillon was a member of one of the leading Anglo-Irish land-owning families, and along with his land, Costello also granted Dillon his chief stronghold, Castlemore.

In 1568 Queen Elizabeth issued instructions granting to Sir Richard Bourke, Earl of Clanrickard, certain lands including "the vicarages of Kylleare, Began and Annagh". Ulick Bourke, his successor, later held land at Kildarra. In 1586 however, Becan was mentioned as part of the estate of 'MacCostello', and it was later granted by King James the First to Theobald Dillon. Dillon's hold on the rest of the local area endured until Michael Davitt's Agrarian Revolution of the early part of the 19th century, when much of the land passed into the hands of the local tenants. The Burke presence, however, persisted, and apparently the Becan townland was held by the Burkes on a lease from Lord Dillon for most of the 19th century. Again, John Francis Burke (Coroner for Mayo in 1844) was mentioned, as was his son Patrick, a doctor at Claremorris, who died in 1891.

The original village of Becan consisted of a group of dwellings near Barry's Well, originally known as MacDonagh's Well, in Brackloon West. Its name in Irish is 'Cnoc na Boithe'. By 1839, the village was in ruins, as is shown on the Ordnance Survey Map of that year. In later years, a permanent school was built for the area on the Spotfield Estate, about a quarter of a mile from where the current school now stands. The Burkes of Becan owned the best of the land, which was at Spotfield, 'from the Lissaniska road on the south to the high road to Knock on the north'. They lived in 'a long thatched house beside the road between the new school and the church'.

The Burke's relationship with the local Catholic Church was interesting, and formative in the history of the family in the area. John Francis Burke, the Coroner of the 1840's, had allowed Canon Peter Geraghty to live in a thatched house on his land. This was the first tenancy of a priest on the land since before the Penal times. The Augustinians had apparently been present in the area before that time. Around the year 1900, the Burke family became impoverished, and was unable to resume management of Becan farm. At that time the Land Commission, finding Canon Geraghty in residence there, recognised him as tenant under the Land Act. Subsequent to a fire at his thatched residence, Fr. Geraghty built the parochial residence called locally "The Priest's". This was a two storey slated house which served his successors until a 'Father White' built the new parochial house in 1932. Six more houses were built by the Congested Districts' Board on the land taken over from the Burkes, and six holdings of land given to tenants around the locality.

The book included a fascinating description of a local feast held every year on the Burkes' farm. This was the feast of 'Saint Beacuan', the patron saint of the parish, and was held on the ninth of July of each year, on the land between the local church and the road to Lissaniska. The celebration was known locally as a "pattern". Whether 'Saint Beacuan' was a real historical figure is thought by some scholars to be questionable.

Other mentions of Burkes in the book included that of Tom Burke having put up three hundred acres of land for sale for twenty four pounds in the Becan area in 1752, and Joseph Burke of Becan having been recorded as a member of the Loughlin Cavalry in 1796. Another Joseph Burke was noted as having been an absentee landlord during the Land War in 1897, and there also was a reference to a Frank Burke having addressed a meeting of the United Irish League in 1904. In the 'Griffith's Valuation' of 1856, the only Burke name recorded was that of John F. Bourke, who owned a house in Becan.

That there had been so much research published in this manner was fortunate. It was certainly an astonishing stroke of luck as overnight I had a picture of Bekan and the Burke family. It was almost too much to take in. It is always gratifying to establish a reliable confirmation of hearsay and be able to record information with confidence.

Later I discovered a statistical survey of Co. Mayo that was carried out in 1801 by James M'Parlan, M.D.[34] and this provided a good picture of the Becan area at the time of James Dominick. M'Parlan's account describes Becan as relatively poor land for farming, being mostly reclaimed bog. What was particularly striking was the picture presented of the degree of poverty endured in the area at the time.

The richest of the yeoman farmers have not a second hearth, nor windows to subject them to that tax, although paying an annual rent of from one to two hundred pounds; the houses are built of stone and dashed with clay mortar and seldom in any of them a chimney. The villagers who are in partnership divide themselves according to their numbers into 4 or 8 parties; each party keeps a horse, the joint property of the whole, which horses do in common the work of the village.

All of this information was fascinating and invaluable, however the jewel of this research was the amazing discovery of an eighteenth century song that had been written in honour of Frank Burke of Becan! It was composed in 1760, and it was called "Plaincsti Bheacain".[35] The following is Nollaig Ó Muraile's translation of the words written to honour this illustrious resident of Becan.[36]

The Bekan Planxty (translation from the Irish)

Let us go over to County Mayo
To the young man who lives in Bekan –
Frank Burke, that gay young blade,
Paragon of beauty and excellence;
With his bright flawless cheeks
And shining blue eyes,
Not a man of renown in all the earth
But gladly admits him to his confidence and friendship.

A while spent in dalliance with white-breasted damsels
A while drinking toasts to the gentry;
A while – without fail – a-hunting on the bogs
Whenever our hero feels lonely;
Then again, to escape, out trampling the hills
With a playful barking dog for company,
While the doe and her young leap over rocks -
He has all the provinces in his sway!

Nollaig Ó Muraile had carried out extensive research into the origins of this song, and guessed that Frank Burke must have been either the father or grandfather of the Joseph Burke listed in the Loughlin Cavalry membership of 1796. This was to remain only a guess however, until he made what was for me one of the most significant discoveries of all. In the issue of 8th to 12th May, 1764, of a Dublin newspaper called Pue's Occurrences, he found the following notice:

Marriages: At Tuam, Mr. Francis Burke of Becane in the Co. of Mayo, to Miss Mary Kirwan, daughter of Richard Kirwan of the Co. Galway, Esq.

This confirmed the probability that Joseph Burke of Becan, a member of the Loughlin Cavalry in 1796, was the son of Frank Burke, and indeed of Mary Kirwan. My great-great grandfather, James Dominick Burke, was born around the year 1780. What could the relationship have been? We were getting tantalisingly close.

Two major objectives were now apparent. One was to establish the relationship between James Dominick and the other Burkes of Becan. The other was to find the connection between the Burkes of Becan and a recognised branch of the Burke clan. This would be considerably more difficult. According to the experts at the South Mayo Family Research Centre, substantial research carried out by professional genealogists over the years had been unable to establish the ancestry of the Becan Burkes. It seemed highly unlikely that I could succeed where they had failed.

[11]
Filling Gaps

Your father had a cousin in London, a retired paymaster from the navy named Walter Burke. Another cousin of your fathers, Bernard Burke was a young officer in the Crimean War and slept in the same tent as Colonel Brennan. He is now stationed in Dublin as Major Burke, paymaster of pensions.

With some experience behind me I was able to go immediately to the better-known centralised records and publications to see if more could be added to the Burke material. Quickly I realised that this was not going to be easy, not because I could find no Burke references, but because there were so many.

The search commenced in a most haphazard manner. In the now familiar archives I looked for wills, marriage licenses, funeral entries and Burke family pedigrees. Newspapers were examined including 'Pue's Occurrences' and 'Dublin Gazette'. commercial directories such as Thoms, Watson's Almanac and Pettigrew & Oulton were discovered and I had to resist the temptation to follow irrelevant yet absorbing entries. I had one find.

The Index to Prerogative Wills of Ireland contained an entry - 1757 Thomas Burke, Becan, Mayo.[37] Unfortunately this was only an index of wills, the originals of which were destroyed in the 1922 fire.[38] The only other Burke I could identify as possibly ours was John F. Bourke, Greenhills, Westport, who was a coroner in 1830. I carefully recorded many references to Burkes in case they became significant at a later stage. This is one of the great difficulties in carrying out research. A record may seem meaningless at the time, yet assume great significance later when more is known. I found reference to a Walter Burke, Paymaster, serving on HM Cressy.[39]

Several aspects of this line of inquiry were intriguing. Clearly the Burke of Ower pedigree was that which Uncle Tom regarded as his line - but why? My father had mentioned the Clanricarde lineage, long before he and I found the Colwyn Bay family tree, and now I wondered from where he had got such an idea. I looked for Christian names that might give a lead and found quite a few Dominicks, one of whom was a Burke of Ower. Could Uncle Tom have noticed this and simply jumped to a wrong conclusion? Surely he would have had better reason than that to assert that it was our line.

I realised that the temptation to research Burke genealogy from the 12th century onwards had to be resisted, for the moment at any rate. Preoccupation with the Burkes of old was unlikely in the short term to help in identifying more recent ancestors. I gathered together my latest notes and returned to Mayo.

The Castlebar public library is modern, bright and includes a most attractive local history section. I began to search through old newspapers for references to the Burke family of Becan. I was happy to find anything new, but also I hoped to fill in some background to what had been provided by the research centre at Ballinrobe. From the Becan book and the records at Ballinrobe I found that John Francis Burke the Coroner had three sons, Dr. John Patrick Burke of Claremorris, James T. Burke, Clerk of the Claremorris Union and Charles Burke of Bekan.

Among the records that I considered to be the most significant were the death notice of John P. Burke, Esq., MD aged 50 years who died on the 28th of August 1891 in Claremorris. His funeral was to take place at the 'family burial ground' in Ballyhaunis. In another newspaper article, this man's father was recorded as John F. Burke, Coroner at Westport, while his grandfather was noted as 'the late John Burke, Esq., of Greenhills'. In the issue of the 5th of September 1891 of the 'Connaught Telegraph', there was a notice of a special meeting of the Claremorris Guardians,[40] 'owing to the death of the late much-lamented Dr. Burke'. The board resolved to send letters of condolence to Dr. Burke's mother, sisters, and two brothers. Also noted from a log of the minutes of a meeting of the board, was the board's acceptance of a solicitor's letter, recorded as follows.

There was a letter from Mr Kirwan, Solicitor, on behalf of Anne Burke, wife of the late Dr Burke, stating that they were married on August 1st 1890 at Christ's Church, Maiden Lane, London, by Rev C Bickley, Catholic Curate, in the presence of Thomas Quinn and Nora Jennings, sister of Mrs Burke. The letter was sent by way of caution to the guardians, lest they should pay the one quarter's salary due to the late Dr Burke to any person other than his lawful wife, Anne Burke.

The Board had sent messages of sympathy to the mother, brothers and sisters of the late doctor, but was unaware that he had married in London a year previously. In a town the size of Claremorris this was surprising indeed. These reports provided food for thought. I had now many leads to follow, including the family burial ground at Ballyhaunis and the record of the doctor's grandfather, John Burke of Greenhills, and was able at this stage to produce the first tentative family tree of the Burkes of Becan.

Not for the first time I looked again at old papers and notes inherited from my father. I had come to regard this as an important practice for the reason already mentioned, that often some piece of information, which originally appeared to be of no interest, could assume great significance later. This is precisely what occurred on this occasion and led to finding another missing piece of the jig-saw.

Among the records inherited from my father were two old diaries, from one of which I had been able to build quite a record of my grandmother Walshe's family. The second diary appeared to be that of Annie Goodwin. It consisted almost entirely of records of births and deaths and was of considerable help in building up the family tree. On re-reading it I came across the following marriage notice taken from a newspaper:

BURKE and COSGROVE - December 13, 1884, at St. Peters Roman Catholic Church, Birmingham, by the Rev. H. D. Ryder, of the Oratory. Major Bernard H. Burke, Staff Officer of Pensioners, late 68th Durham Light Infantry, to Constance, widow of the late John Cosgrove, and daughter of E. Edden, of West Grove, Edgbaston.

Annie's letter referred to her cousin Bernard Burke who had served in Crimea. My father had followed this up, and obtained a marriage certificate from Birmingham of one Bernard Hamilton Burke. However, this record did not seem to fit in with Annie's cousin, as Bernard would have been only seventeen years of age at Crimea.

Now however, with this new record, I changed my opinion. Surely this had to be "Cousin Bernard", or why had the notice been kept by one of the family? Among notes we had taken at the Public Record Office at Kew many years previously we recorded various entries relating to a Bernard H. Burke between the years 1857 and 1886, all with military connotations. Clearly this related to the man married in Birmingham.

I decided to try another approach. The marriage certificate showed Bernard's father to be a Francis Burke, physician.[41] If the families were related, then there was a reasonable chance that they came originally from the Becan area. So I asked the

Mercer library to look for records of Burke doctors from that part of Mayo in the mid-nineteenth century. The findings were even better than I could have expected. Not only was there a Dr. Francis Burke practising in Westport in 1850, but also, in the same town, lived a Dr. Thomas Hamilton Burke!

The Church of Ireland registers at the South Mayo Family Research Centre contained a record of the marriage of Francis Burke and Margaret Hamilton in 1821. They also had a record the death of Thomas Hamilton who was buried in November 1830, aged 71 years.

We found that Dr. Francis Burke was eighty-two years of age when he died in 1877 and that his wife Mary Burke (formerly Hamilton) was 79 years when she died in 1883. They lived in Octagon House in the centre of Westport. Of the children, the most notable was Dr. Thomas Hamilton Burke who died in Dublin in 1898 and had a large family.

The doctors Francis Burke and Thomas Hamilton were recorded as having been buried at Oughaval graveyard, three miles west of Westport. Oughaval, now Westport, takes its name from the church whose ruins are still evident in the graveyard. With the aid of a map provided by my Ballinrobe friends we found the graves of Doctor Thomas Hamilton, who died on the 21st of October 1830, and Francis Burke, M.D., who died on the 17th of August 1877. They are buried side by side with their gravestones still quite legible. Later I found records of their wills in the National Archives.

The conclusive proof of the connection between the Hamilton Burkes of Westport and the Burkes of Becan came in the following extract from the Connaught Telegraph of 17th March 1883:

DEATH OF MRS BURKE on the 15th at her residence, The Octagon House, Westport, Margaret Hamilton, relict of the late Francis Burke, Esq., M.D., aged 79 years. In her last minutes she had the consolation of being surrounded by several members of her much respected and truly amiable family. Three of her sons, Dr Thos Burke, Inspector of L G Board, J W Burke, Esq. R N, and Capt. B H Burke, staff officer Pensioners &c., while her other two surviving sons, Dr F Nail Burke, and General J W Burke occupy the highest positions of respectability and trust in America, the latter being General in command of the United States Army Mobile. On yesterday, Friday, the remains of the much-lamented lady were borne for internment to the family burial vault, Oughavale cemetery, followed by a large concourse of sorrowing friends. The chief mourners on the sad and eventful occasion were her three sons aforementioned - E Gaffney, Esq., Revisor; Jas T Burke, and Chas Burke, Claremorris. A large contingent of the Connaught Rangers attended to convey the coffin to and from the hearse.

This confirmed that Bernard was a son of the deceased, and that James T. Burke and Charles Burke of Claremorris, whom we now knew to be Becan Burkes, were related to the Hamilton Burkes. Again, the details of Annie's letter were correct.

Solving this puzzle provided real satisfaction and, of course, was a reminder of the benefit of pursuing all leads. Had I not come across a small cutting in a very old diary we might never have known about our Hamilton Burke cousins. In much the same way an old envelope had led us to the Creaghs. We were still finding answers in the most unlikely of places, as Hugh Lees had predicted many years ago.

I eventually located the Will of Bernard Hamilton Burke in the Will Index Catalogue in the National Archives which in turn led me to an entry in the Census of Ireland 1911,[32] showing that he had retired to Rosbeg, Westport as Lieutenant Colonel. He died in 1916, leaving four daughters. His brother John had been in residence at Octagon House in Westport after the death of their mother, and died there in 1901. Octagon House was the Hamilton Burke family home.

Fig. 11   COLLIS FAMILY

Rev. Samuel of Fort William

m. Anna Rae Langford of Gardensfield, Co. Limerick

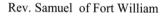

William of Fort William	Catherine	Samuel	Ellen
	b.1778	of the Spa	
m.1814 Deborah Crumpe (1)	m.1806 William Collis	m. C.Lyne	m. Francis
m.1830 Louisa Emma Burke (2)	her 1st cousin		Collingwood
			Capt. R.N.

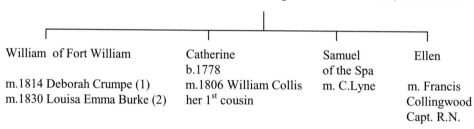

marriage (1)   marriage (2)

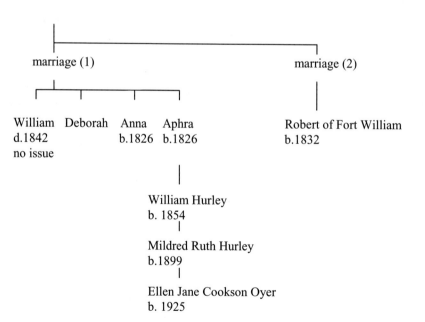

William	Deborah	Anna	Aphra	Robert of Fort William
d.1842		b.1826	b.1826	b.1832
no issue				

William Hurley
b. 1854

Mildred Ruth Hurley
b.1899

Ellen Jane Cookson Oyer
b. 1925

[12]
Louisa Emma

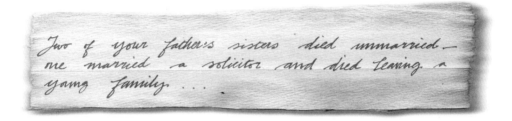

Two of your father's sisters died unmarried — one married a solicitor and died leaving a young family . . .

Whereas Connaught in general, and Galway and Mayo in particular, were identified with the ancestry of the Burkes, County Kerry had been home to the Collingwoods and Collises. I decided to make yet another trip to Kerry in pursuit of Collis records, although I accepted this was unlikely to help in the quest for my Burke ancestry.

To find Fort William would be important, if only to photograph the Collis ancestral home. As in-laws of Francis Collingwood, it seemed appropriate to take more than a passing interest in the family. Indeed it occurred to me that I should start building a Collis tree, bearing in mind the connection between the Collises and the Collingwoods. Perhaps these were just excuses at the time as, to be honest, I was enjoying the field trips even when they produced nothing by way of progress. I was meeting people, learning much by way of local history and folklore, and was exploring countryside often way off the beaten track.

Discipline was needed, so as usual I did some homework before setting off. In order to get an idea of the Collis family history, I decided to take notes from the 1868 edition of Burkes Landed Gentry that I assumed would include reference to the marriage of Ellen Collis and Francis Collingwood. I had to read the entry for 'Collis of Fort William' twice before I realised what I had discovered. The entry showed that Robert Collis was living at Fort William in 1868. It stated that Robert was the grandson of the Reverend Samuel Collis and Anna Rae Langford, among whose daughters was listed Ellen Collis, who married Francis Collingwood. The entry then referred to the eldest son of Samuel Collis, whose name was William, 'captain and adjutant of the Royal Kerry Militia' (Fig.11). William was first married in 1814, to a lady by the name of Deborah, the daughter of William John

Crumpe Esq., MD of Tralee, by whom he had three daughters, and a son, William. Robert, however, was the product of William's second marriage, which was entered as follows:

Mr Collis m. 2ndly in 1830 (22 Nov) Louisa-E, dau of Dr. Burke, R.N., Co. Wexford and by her had a son, Robert, present representative.

At first I thought I was seeing things - that I had copied the Creagh family in error. But no, Emma had married William Collis, brother of Ellen and brother-in-law of Emma's uncle, Francis Collingwood, before she married Michael Creagh! This was extraordinary. Did the Creagh descendants in New Zealand know that their Burke ancestor was not only a widow when she married Michael Creagh, but that she had also produced a Collis heir before the death of her first husband? Her son Robert Collis was presumably Louisa Jane's first grandchild and was still living at Fort William in 1868. He had inherited his father's seat at Fort William only upon the death of his older half brother. Robert's father died in 1834, and his half-brother William died in 1842.

The implications of what I had found took time to sink in. One could but speculate on the circumstances of Emma's first encounter with the widower William Collis. Presumably Emma had accompanied her mother and stepfather Mullay to Wexford with the other children. Alternatively it was conceivable that she had gone to live with the Collingwoods in Tralee following the death of her father, James Dominick, in 1822. One way or another, she had met and been married to William Collis as a very young girl. Now there was an entirely new dimension to my forthcoming trip to Kerry.

It occurred to me that the Collis-Burke wedding might have taken place in the Wexford parish where Louisa Jane and Mullay were living. I went back to the notes taken on my very first visit to Wexford – and there it was in black and white. Once again I found notes that had previously been considered to be of no significance emerging as vital clues at a later stage in the game. I had taken down all of the marriage records that related to the names Burke, Mulloy and Mullay from the Wexford area between 1691 and 1845, a total of over thirty entries. I had not, of course, recognised the entry "Louisa Emma and William Collis, 1830" for its true significance, having been unaware at the time of either of the names.

The "Wexford Herald" newspaper provided more details. In the edition of the 20th of November 1830 was the following notice:

Married on the 18th instant in Killinick Church, by the Rev. Mr. Reade, William Collis of Fort William, in the County of Kerry, Esq., to Louisa Emma, 2nd daughter of the late James D Burke, M.D.

The "Kerry Evening Post" of 22nd November also covered the marriage and described Louisa Emma Burke as a niece of 'Collingwood of the Spa'. Now we knew that Emma was married in 1830 in the Wexford Church of Ireland parish of Killinick, and that at the time the Collingwoods were living at the Spa, near Tralee. This raised further questions. Louisa Jane had married Mullay in 1828, so they must have moved to Wexford quite soon after the wedding. Could Emma's marriage have been "arranged", possibly by Louisa Jane, who would have recognised the wealth and reputation of the Collis family? Did Emma inherit wealth on the death of her husband or did it all pass from one son to the other? Before trying to answer these questions, it seemed sensible to find out what I could about the Collis family and about the Irish branch of the Collingwoods.

The Kerry County Library is situated in Tralee and, as I found in Castlebar, boasted an impressive local history section. The county of Kerry is particularly well provided with historical books and records. 'Irish Records' by James Ryan and John Grenham's 'Tracing Your Irish Ancestors' list local sources of information for each county, and this is of great help when concentrating on a particular area of the country. I found that while the Collingwoods were hardly documented, the Collis family history was quite easily assembled.

The Collis name is of English origin, deriving from Nicholas, and its establishment in Ireland dates from the middle of the seventeenth century. Two army officers obtained land under the Cromwellian Settlement, and their families settled in the counties of Sligo and Kerry. Whereas the Sligo family appeared to have died out, the Kerry family increased and prospered (Fig.12). Already by 1661 one Collis had become provost of Tralee, and another was listed as a County Kerry Titulado in the census of 1659. From that time until the changes effected by the Land Acts of 1870 to 1903 the Collises of West Munster frequently occupied prominent positions, another example being that of High Sheriff of Kerry. The number of Collis wills proved in the Prerogative court between 1685 and 1857 testified to their continued prosperity. In 1878 they owned twelve thousand acres in counties Kerry, Cork, Limerick and Tipperary. Emma had obviously married well.

This second trip to Kerry was a great success. Further computer printouts from the Church of Ireland in Tralee showed a number of Collis baptisms, marriages and deaths, and included the marriage in the Ballymacelligott Union of 'Louisa Emma Collis to Michael Creagh on 24th May 1843', which included a note to the effect that Emma was a widow.

We found the church at Ballymacelligott, which we had learned from the Church of Ireland in Tralee was the building used for the marriage of Emma to Michael. The church was still standing, still in use, and in good condition, having been built in

Fig. 12   COLLIS LINEAGE

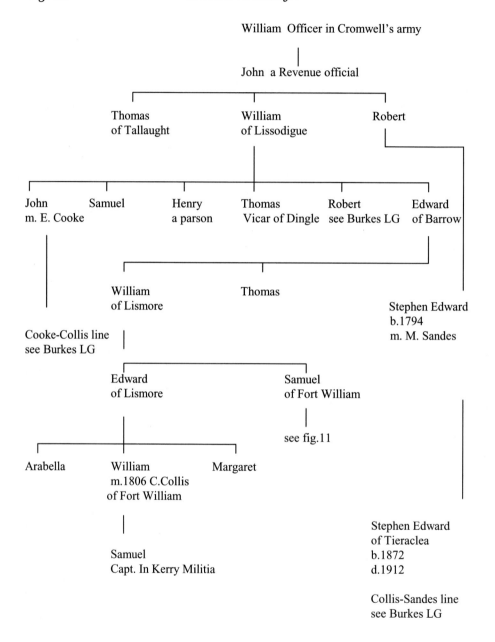

William Officer in Cromwell's army

John a Revenue official

Thomas   William   Robert
of Tallaught   of Lissodigue

John   Samuel   Henry   Thomas   Robert   Edward
m. E. Cooke   a parson   Vicar of Dingle see Burkes LG   of Barrow

                        William   Thomas
                        of Lismore
                                                                      Stephen Edward
                                                                      b.1794
Cooke-Collis line   m. M. Sandes
see Burkes LG

            Edward   Samuel
            of Lismore   of Fort William

                                            see fig.11

Arabella   William   Margaret
                m.1806 C.Collis
                of Fort William

                                                                      Stephen Edward
                                                                      of Tieraclea
            Samuel   b.1872
            Capt. In Kerry Militia   d.1912

                                                                      Collis-Sandes line
                                                                      see Burkes LG

1824 on the site of the old parish church. We visited the Ballynahagilish cemetery at Churchill, on the road from Tralee to Barrow, where many of the Collis family are buried, and also Barrow House, the home of one branch of the Collises. We also saw Kent Lodge, situated at Spa, nearer to Tralee, another Collis residence in the last century.

The highlight of the visit was finding the place that had for so long eluded us. Fort William, a townland not shown on the current Ordinance Survey map, is located a few miles from Abbeydorney. The present owner took us to view what was left of the property. We were taken across fields and through gates on a sunny summer's day, way off the beaten track. The entrance was at the beginning of a long avenue which led to the side of the house and courtyard. The house was built in 1780 and is now almost a ruin. The Collis name can be seen over the original doorway. We were shown where the soldiers of the Royal Kerry Militia were accommodated in out-houses close to the ruins of the horses' stables. The property is situated on the highest point of the surrounding rather flat countryside, from which one can see great distances in every direction. It was from this house that Ellen Collis came, marrying Captain Francis Collingwood in 1822, and it was to this house that Emma Burke came to live eight years later.

Returning to Dublin I decided to check at the Registry of Deeds[9] for a record of Emma Burke's marriage to William Collis. After all, the Collis family was likely to have entered into a marriage settlement or perhaps transferred some property on the marriage of William Collis to his second wife. Fortunately, as it turned out, I could not remember offhand the year of marriage but, thinking it was 1836, I searched the index, and there it was! Although the marriage was in fact in 1830, the deed was dated 1836. It would appear that the original deed was lost or mislaid and never registered, and that this was a sworn copy made after Collis's death. I would probably never have come across it but for my error in recalling the year of their marriage.

The deed itself was a wonderful find. Not only does it include various family names and their locations, but it also reintroduced Walter Burke as clearly a close family relative. Walter Burke, 'Purser in the Royal Navy', acted as witness to the marriage. Thomas Macnamara Russell was in Belfast at the time, Francis Collingwood at Spa, Tralee, and the Deed itself was executed in Wexford. No doubt Louisa Jane was keeping a close eye on things and ensuring the well-being of her daughter should she predecease her much older husband – the deed arranged that, in the event of the death of William Collis, £100 a year would be paid to Louisa Emma, 'by equal half yearly Portions on every first day of May and first day of November in each year'. The memorial of the deed, which I had found, was itself witnessed by Benjamin Vicary and Samuel Aitken of Wexford, the latter being apparently a cabinet-maker.

All sorts of questions arose as a result of this find and it was an opportunity to put into practice my determination to focus on just what might lead to a breakthrough in establishing the relationship of James Dominick to the Burkes of Becan and, even more importantly, the connection between the Becan Burkes and the Burkes of Ower. Establishing both links would give us a line back to Charlemagne and the search would be complete - or so I thought at the time.

Contemplating the background to these ancestors and realising my interest now extended beyond the simple compilation of statistics, I thought often about the circumstances surrounding the various events and in particular the lives of Louisa Jane, her daughter Emma and, of course, Annie Goodwin. I was reminded of the following quotation from Michael Coady's book *All Souls.*[60]

The purpose of genealogy should not be the neat assembly of pedigree culminating smugly in self, but its exact opposite: the extension of the personal beyond the self to encounter the intimate unknown of others in our blood.

I had already concluded that the lives of the women in our family were a great deal more interesting than those of the men. Often the husbands married late and died early, leaving a widow to bring up the children. This phenomenon has persisted in our family – from the time of James Dominick in the eighteenth century, my own children have been the first in the male line to know their grandfather! Another surprising fact was that in the same two-hundred-year period, Emma was the only female Burke to have married. We know that her sisters Maria and Catherine died unmarried, and the absence of any reference to Stephania other than that of her birth suggests likewise. The next generation produced four boys including my grandfather. He had two daughters, neither of whom married. My father had three boys only. My wife and I have five children of which only the three boys are married. Our four female grandchildren have some way to go before attempting to break with the tradition. So Emma, as far as we knew, was the only female in two hundred years of my particular Burke line to marry.

Two contacts that I made with distant relatives during this period proved to be highly rewarding. While researching in Tralee I was told about research similar to my own that had been carried out by a visitor from the United States who had been to the area on a number of occasions. She was the great-great granddaughter of William Collis, the first son of Robert's father and was able to provide many details of the history of her side of the family. Equally, I was able to provide her with the details amassed by myself. She sent me a wonderful description of her first visit to Tralee in 1969 when she found Fort William, Barrow House and the Collis vault at Churchill cemetery. Her final comment was, rather sadly, how she wished she could have found a relative who was still alive. However, as she said in her letter, the nicest aspect of the search is getting to know the local people still living.

The second contact that I made was with the son of Edric Collingwood Creagh. Edric was the grandson of Michael Creagh and Louisa Emma, and had been born in 1882. Edric had taken a keen interest in genealogy and I wrote to his son, then in his eightieth year, in New Zealand. I told him of my search, what I had found out about the Burkes and the Creaghs, asking if he had anything to add. In the letter I received back he wrote about Louisa Emma's daughter, Louisa, born in November 1852, who dicd the following month and is buried in the same grave as her mother at Mount Jerome Cemetery in Dublin City. He also told me of a Spanish dirk, a family heirloom won by Francis Collingwood at Trafalgar passed on to Louisa Emma. However, above all this was the following:

My wife and I have a treasured oil painting of Louisa Emma Creagh, nee Burke, about 30 x 24 inches, in an ornate gilt frame, artist unknown and not signed. She has dark blue eyes, fair complexion with rosy cheeks, auburn hair with long curls down each side of her face. She is wearing an off the shoulder black dress and with what appears to be an ostrich feather stole. She has no rings on her fingers, which may indicate that she was painted before her marriage. Around her neck and reaching perhaps to waist level is a fine long gold chain which she is fingering. A circular brooch with diamonds is on the neckline of her dress.

[13]
The Abbey at Ballyhaunis

In olden times people did not distinguish the graves of their dead by setting up inscribed tombstones bearing epitaphs or appropriate details, except perhaps in the case of a powerful chieftain or a very distinguished personage. The ordinary people died, were buried and then forgotten after a little while, at the longest when those who had known them personally during life followed them in the course of nature to the earthly homes of everlasting silence. What an amount of history lies buried in all these unused graveyards throughout the district; what tragedy, romance, heroism, glory or misery, who can tell? God alone knows! - 'Antiquarian' Connaught Telegraph, 1937

At one o'clock in the afternoon of the 29th of August 1891, the remains of Dr. John Patrick Burke left the house in Claremorris for burial in the family vault in the grounds of the Augustinian Friary in Ballyhaunis. He was the last of the Burkes of Bekan to be buried there. Some time later the present church was built over part of the old graveyard including the area of tombs and vaults and so, for the last hundred years or so, the vault has been sealed off.

This information emerged after a number of visits to the Friary. But perhaps it is best to begin with some historical background information on the Abbey, which I learned largely from the Becan book.[31]

The Abbey was established by the descendants of the local Lord, Costello, around the year 1430. Until the early 17th century, it existed in relative peace. At this time the Abbey was suppressed by occupying forces. In spite of this interference the life of the Abbey persisted until it was raided by a garrison of parliamentary troops from Dunmore. The troops set fire to the building, and hanged both the prior, Fr. Fulgentius Jordan, and another Friar Fulgentius, who was nicknamed 'Béalórga' or 'Golden Mouth' for his eloquence at the pulpit. Béalórga is said to have been "dragged from the pulpit as he was exhorting the people to stand firm". The two were hanged from a tree in the grounds of the Abbey, and once the soldiers were gone, their bodies were buried in the vault that is underneath the present sacristy.

The typed papers of L.W. Carr O.S.A. from1937 referred to a draft history of burials of Friars and others dating back to 1616.[42] These made mention of the 'Vault of the Burkes of Baken',[31] and located it 'Under the threshold of the door of the side porch'. The papers also referred to the vault of the Burkes of Holywell, which is at the east end of the church. Indeed parts of Fr. Carr's account of the graveyard were quite disturbing.

The area round the Abbey is full of graves. Right out to the edge of the hill over looking the river and for all we know further. When digging to place the gate leading out to the hill path down to the bridge human bones were found in great quantities many feet down below the present ground level.

Having found the church and the graveyard, it was frustrating to think that the vault was there but inaccessible. The Abbey is a haven of peace with an avenue of trees leading up from the town of Ballyhaunis. My interest in burials, graveyards, vaults and the like had been growing for some time and the Abbey not only reminded me of this, but also generated thoughts about the ordinary people who lived in bygone days and went to their final resting place in the grounds.

Some might regard these as rather gloomy thoughts. On the other hand, if one is to take an interest in family history, it is an inescapable fact that those we are researching are dead and gone. That is unless you believe in ghosts – a subject that has not been omitted entirely from my story. The truth is that these days I enjoy wandering around cemeteries, reading the tombstones and imagining the circumstances of the lives of those interred – often these can be determined from just a short engraving on a headstone. Occasionally, however, I feel I am trespassing on the private affairs of long-dead strangers.

There were a number of books and documents on the subject of the Friary and the Augustinian vault, but it was from "Antiquarian" in the *Connaught Telegraph* that I found the most appropriate comments.

From an article written in 1937 I learned that, while an enclosed graveyard had been set up near the house of residence, the actual burial area had extended far beyond the limits of that early graveyard, to include 'countless thousands' of graves.[43] The walls of this graveyard have long since collapsed, and the tombstones are at this stage buried. Many of the graves, however, would not have had stones to mark them – the location of burial being held sacred in the memories of those who remained, and who mourned their dead in prayer at the grave-site. The little cemetery was only closed for internment fifty years before the article was written, although it is hardly recognisable as a graveyard at this stage.

The article also gave an account of a development project on the church that had been undertaken at the time by 'Fr. Mansfield, O.S.A'. During the course of the excavations for the foundations of a new sacristy, the workmen came across a dramatic vault.

After digging down some feet, the workmen came to a massive rectangular stone, devoid of all names, dates, marks or symbols of any kind. On the stone being removed an opening was disclosed from which four or five stone steps led down to the entrance to a vault, finely built of stone and mortar, perfectly arched, with three little recesses in each of the side walls and one in the gable. Stretched on the floor were several complete skeletons, while in the wall recesses were skulls and human bones. Nothing was discovered to show whose were the remains enclosed in this dismal underground tomb, and it was evident that the last internment must have been a long time ago. Inquiry was set on foot to discover if the vault might belong to any local family, but no helpful information was forthcoming in that direction. The site of Lord Dillon's vault is well known, and so is that of the Burkes of Holywell and the Burkes of Bekan.

The vault was built beneath the known site of Lord Dillon's vault, suggesting that it was of a very great age indeed. The article surmised that it could well have been the burial vault of some of the early Augustinians, possibly the martyred Fr. Fulgentius Jordan.

Father John O'Connor spent many years at the Abbey in Ballyhaunis and both of us shared a common interest in its history, particularly in the vaults. He kindly copied and gave me notes taken over the years by various members of the community who were engaged in searching for the graves of members of the order. He had written the story of the Abbey, published by the Augustinian Community, and was interested to see if the vaults could be re-examined. In 1932 research and exhumations took place in connection with the cause of the Irish Augustinian Martyrs and in particular the Venerable Fulgentius who was hanged in the grounds in the seventeenth century. In 1937, when excavating to lay foundations for the new sacristy, more details were recorded of what was found. Apparently one theory was advanced that the vault could have been that of the Burkes of Becan. The story of how this question was resolved was fascinating.

It was suggested that [the vault] might be that of the Burkes of Bekan. An old blind man of very advanced years was called who had assisted at the last burial made in the Burke vault. Being left to his own devices he stood at length over the spot where the vault of the Burkes of Bekan was said by others to be, i.e. on the left of the threshold of the entrance to the side porch of the church. He was very positive that no vault was known in his time to exist on the spot where the newly discovered one was found.

Somewhere under or beside the foundations of the present church lies the vault of the Burkes of Becan, which presumably was closed but visible from the outside up to the nineteen thirties. Who knows what might be revealed if we could re-open it. Father O'Connor and I share this interest in further excavations, he to find Fulgentius Jordan and I to find my ancestors. Since then we have kept in touch, particularly since the Order's decision to depart from Ballyhaunis. What this will lead to remains to be seen. One hopes for the preservation of the church and its grounds, including the graveyard. Selfishly I wonder if it might provide an opportunity to open the vault. In another of Fr. Carr's notes I had been given a tantalising impression of what lay beneath the side entrance to the church:

Fr. Edward O'Flynn O.S.A. died 11 Aug.1942 buried in community plot above Fr. Nolan who died 11 Feb.1919. When excavating the grave for Fr. O'Flynn, the vault of the Burkes of Bekan was disclosed and a breastplate showed that the last internment in the Burke vault was in 1891 (Dr. Burke). Several steps led down to the vault.

[14]
Ghosts

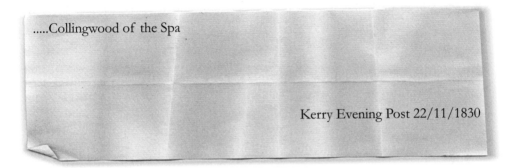

.....Collingwood of the Spa

Kerry Evening Post 22/11/1830

This preoccupation of mine with graves, tombs and the dead was not confined to my Mayo ancestors – indeed some of the more involving incidents took place in the county of Kerry, and none more surprising than when I decided to take a particular interest in properties rather than people.

The notes I had recorded on previous visits to Kerry from a variety of sources mentioned a number of houses, such as Barrow House, Kent Lodge, Fort William, Lismore and others. Oddly enough it was through my newly acquired interest in these houses that certain stories emerged, some reliable, others, I am sure, part of the Kerry folklore. I am indebted to a number of people in the Tralee area whose interest in local history proved invaluable in tracking down records of Collingwoods and Collises and of course it was through them that I eventually located these houses.

The first we visited was Barrow House. My wife and I had been to Barrow House previously on the occasion of a wedding reception, but at the time I was unaware that it was built by John Collis in 1650. It remained in the Collis family for centuries and was occupied by a descendant, another John Collis, around 1822. Situated beside Barrow Harbour, it is a few miles from Fenit and Ardfert.

Of greater significance to our story is Kent Lodge located on the coast road between Tralee and Fenit, in the townland of Ballygarran ('the town of the shrubbery'). We enjoyed the hospitality of the owner on a number of occasions, and were shown around the house. From Valerie Bary's book *Houses of Kerry*,[44] which referred to the house as being of 'great character and atmosphere', I learned some of the details of its history. The house had originally been called 'O'Connell's Cottage', and families associated with the house had included Collis, Collingwood and Stokes.

Kent Lodge was built onto the original building, O'Connell's Cottage, which ultimately made for a very large house, standing flat against the road. The design of the south side of the house is a blend of Regency and Irish country style, including beehive roofs and a large Venetian-style window with some coloured glass, and the whole building is painted 'a striking Venetian red'.

The house was built by Major William Collis, a first cousin of the Reverend Samuel Collis of Fort William, who named the house after the Duke of Kent, son of George III and father of Queen Victoria. Major Collis had lost his right arm defending the Duke during a mutiny at Malta, and was granted a large pension in his retirement for the loss. The story of the Major's death was an unusual one.

In 1821 he was murdered by a gang who broke into his house, having heard of a large amount of money he was said to have held in his desk. He bravely resisted the attack, recognising the men and calling out their names. Two of these turned King's Evidence and, with the evidence given by Mrs Collis, three were convicted of murder and were hanged and one escaped and enlisted abroad.

After the Major's death, Francis Collingwood and Ellen Collis took up residence at Kent Lodge. This was the house in which Francis and Ellen brought up their children and lived for many years. Francis died in 1835, after which George Collingwood Vigors Stokes took up residence at the Lodge, this name suggesting yet another relationship.

The Major's presence has not, however, been entirely forgotten. According to the Bary book, the present owners 'admit that they sometimes hear the Major around the house, but that he is a friendly visitor'. I had this confirmed for me upon my own visit, when I learned that heavy footsteps are heard on the stairs every August and that a military or naval hand and wrist have been seen and described in great detail. Although a friendly-ghost, a member of the family was thrown out of bed on one occasion! I expected all of this to remain a mere story, but I cannot say that such has entirely been the case.

We checked all of the properties that Valerie Bary had researched, and which were included in her book. There we found two further houses which were at one time occupied by Collingwoods, almost a century before the marriage of Francis and Ellen! Until now, I had assumed that Francis was the first Collingwood to take up residence in Ireland in 1822.

The first of these was 'Ardraw House' located off the Killorglin-Beaufort road, and in ruin. The house was very old, and may have been built by the Collingwoods. Once again, it was believed locally that Ardraw house was haunted.

The second was Collingwood House, situated at Knockane, Beaufort the structure of which indicated that it was built in the seventeenth or early eighteenth centuries, the windows being built close to the corners of the house. It was still inhabited, and had been held by farming families from the time of the Collingwoods to the present time. Bary noted that the house had remained almost untouched, retaining its 'historical character'.

The first of a number of strange incidents occurred when, accompanied by my wife, I went to locate and view the two houses. I recorded the events as coincidental but others have considered the explanation to be deeper than that. We decided to look for Ardraw House first, it being situated on one side of the Killorglin to Beaufort road. We agreed to leave the Collingwood house until the following day.

Finding Ardraw proved difficult. Local residents did not seem to have heard of it, which was not surprising really, the house having been derelict and unoccupied for many years. Eventually we came across a house with yellow gateposts that we assumed, for some reason, to be Ardraw. We drove up a long avenue and around to a yard at the back of the house. Only then did we notice a light inside, shining through a small window at the rear. It was occupied! I suppose in earlier days I would have summoned up courage and knocked on the side door, but not on this occasion. We immediately drove out again, remarking that either we were at the wrong house or that it was true what was said about the haunting! Bary's book includes a sketch of each building, and when we looked back from the road it was obvious that we were mistaken – this was not Ardraw House.

Further enquiry revealed the location of Ardraw to be many miles from where we had been searching. It was reputed to be four hundred years old and looked to be in a very bad state of repair. We spoke with the present owners who knew nothing of the Collingwoods, other than one who recalled that a Collingwood had been living in the Tralee area about one hundred years ago.

The following day we set out to find Collingwood House and this proved even more difficult. With the help of the post office in Killorglin, some local historians and a telephone call to Valerie Bary, we established a detailed description of the location of the house. It was apparently in a remote region and well off the main road. We eventually found it after much searching – and before us was the house with the yellow gateposts!

The unsettling nature of these events in Kerry revived my memory of a similar occurrence that had taken place, also in Kerry, long before I set out on my search for ancestors. I had also been reminded of this incident when I found the grave of Louisa Jane next to the farmhouse where we had spent our summer holidays many years previously, both located just across the road from Evelyne Miller's home. Certain events may be described as coincidental, but this story defied a logical explanation.

In the early seventies, I returned to Dublin, having spent four years living in Essex and working in London. During those four years a difficulty had often arisen when talking to people about Ireland. Everyone had heard of Killarney, many had visited there and, naturally, were taken with the beauty of the surrounding area. Unfortunately, although we had travelled to various parts of the country as children and teenagers, I had never made it to Kerry. The English, and particularly the Americans, could not understand this, and so after a while I lied and agreed with them on the beauty of Killarney, the lakes and mountains! It was easier than telling the truth!

A year or so after I returned to Ireland, my job took me around the country to visit doctors in general practice. This entailed setting up appointments, allowing about two hours for each. One day I had an appointment arranged in Kenmare at ten o'clock in the morning, followed by another in the early evening in Tralee. However, when I arrived in Kenmare I found out that my appointment had been cancelled. So I set off for Tralee on a bright sunny day, realising that I would get there a few hours early. As this was my first time in the county of Kerry, I decided that, rather than hang around Tralee for hours, I would go via Killarney and, once and for all, eliminate that embarrassing omission from my experiences as a genuine Irishman.

As I approached Killarney the sky darkened and I arrived in a downpour so heavy that it was impossible to leave the car without getting thoroughly wet. I was in my best business suit, properly attired for my appointments, and could not risk a soaking, so I drove slowly through Killarney and out the other side. It was a real anti-climax after all my discussions with foreigners but, although I saw no lakes or mountains because of the rain, I could now relax in the knowledge that, like everyone else, I had been to Killarney.

Back on the Tralee road the clouds lifted and within minutes the sun was out again as bright as ever. Unfortunately I was set to arrive at my destination several hours too early. At a crossroads I stopped and went into a small shop. An elderly lady served me and in an attempt to engage in conversation that might pass the time, I said this was my first visit to her part of the world. (I remembered my mother telling me that she used to come to Kerry on her holidays as a young child, although to what part I did not know. She was a Dublin woman, now living in London, but I knew her family was originally from Kerry, so she may have stayed with cousins of some sort.) To liven up the conversation, I gave the impression that my mother used to visit this part of the county. More lies! The shopkeeper was interested and enquired about my mother, whose maiden name was Florence O'Mahony. Misunderstanding what I said, she assumed that my mother was born in the county, even though I tried to tell her otherwise. Anyhow, I was told that there were many Florence O'Mahonys in Kerry, both male and female, but that if I took the road to the left which led to Firies and another small road off that one I would come to a railway cottage, and there I would find a man who knew all about the O'Mahonys.

It was such a beautiful summer day that I decided to drive to the O'Mahony expert and, rather than explain why I was there, go along with the story that my mother was from Kerry. It was easier this way, although rather reminiscent of my deviousness in England some years earlier! I found the isolated cottage and was invited in and offered a cup of tea. The woman of the house, very old, sat in front of a small turf fire while her husband made the tea. I realised that despite the sun and warmth of the day, the room was dark and cold. The house consisted of one room only, with a sort of loft area, which was apparently the sleeping quarters. Although probably common in many rural areas, I had never seen anything like it before and overall I found the atmosphere to be a bit creepy. The conversation did nothing to reassure me.

The old lady told me about her last visit to the "city" in the nineteen forties. At first I assumed that she was speaking of Dublin. Then I realised she was referring to Killarney. She had not been out of the immediate locality for almost thirty years! Her husband talked to me about the O'Mahonys, having assumed that I was on the trail of my mother's people, and I remember him literally punching my arm with his fist to emphasise whatever point he was making. By this time I was much too scared to admit that my mother was from Dublin and that I was just trying to fill in time on a business trip. He told me that if I took the road to the left I would come to an O'Mahony farm in a place called Ballybane. Eventually I managed to get out of the house, but he accompanied me to the gate to make sure that I continued up the road, almost as if he suspected me of some sort of deception. I was so relieved to get away that I gladly took off to the left, wondering, as I rubbed my aching arm, where this was all going to end.

I had not realised how isolated some Irish dwellings are. In the Scottish highlands you can travel for miles before coming across the next cottage, but I had not realised that this was also the case in certain parts of rural Ireland. As I made my way up this back road, I saw the farm in the distance and it was then that I began to wonder what was happening. I stopped the car and got out and looked across the fields. It was a familiar sight. I had seen the farm before!

How could this be? Could I have seen a photograph as a child? I had made up the story of my mother coming from Kerry, so this could not be the explanation. I remember well that it was the strangest of feelings to see a familiar house in a place I had never been to in my life.

There was smoke coming from the chimney, although the farmyard was deserted, without a sign of an animal or of any form of machinery. It could almost have been described as derelict. I slowly drove in and around the yard until I was close to the door of the farmhouse. The door was opened a fraction and an old woman stuck her head out. I stayed in the car, as I did not want to frighten her, and lowered the window. She looked at me for a while and then asked, "are you an O'Mahony?" Dumbstruck, I nodded, and the door was opened to me. I can well recall stepping out of the car and into about a foot of wet muck caused by the heavy shower earlier in the day. I went in the door and the lady of the house explained to me that her husband was ill in bed upstairs. I told her who I was, and she asked me if my mother still wore ringlets! She still saw my mother, now in her seventies and living outside London, as a twelve-year old girl who came to their farm for summer holidays. Her husband was Connie O'Mahony, a first cousin of my mother's and the nephew of my grandfather!

As I drove back to Tralee on that summer day I realised for the first time what it felt like to experience something completely inexplicable. I tried to rationalise the situation – perhaps I had seen a photograph of the farmhouse as a child that my mother had kept among her old holiday prints, or perhaps…what? I just could not accept as a mere coincidence that I had happened to stop in Farranfore, had seen a familiar sight in a place that I had never been to and had ended up in the farmhouse where my grandfather was born.

Later, my mother explained that Connie was her father's nephew who had remained on the farm. She had not been in contact with him for many years. She was unaware of any photographs of the place.

More recently I returned to find the farmhouse uninhabited, although I could still make out the yard and the front door from which it was enquired of me if I was an O'Mahony. I suppose that I must have borne some resemblance to my mother, although until then I had never noticed it. Twenty-five years later I was to find out more about the farm and its occupants when my research for my ancestors extended to my mother's family.

Back in Tralee I was told stories about the man in the railway cottage, and how he could gather rats around him by whistling. Apparently they came down the chimney and in through the doors and windows. The old lady was his mother, not his wife. No wonder I sensed an unusual atmosphere, although in retrospect I suppose he was simply showing me hospitality and was glad of a caller and some conversation.

Having returned to Dublin after our visit to the houses of Tralee, and in the context of these strange occurrences, I was naturally interested to hear how the Major behaved following our visit to Kent Lodge. You will recall that his ghostly appearances were confined each year to a short period during August. On this occasion the owner told me that she felt his presence when dried flowers began swaying in a cold breeze on the landing, followed by a few bleeps of the smoke alarm! There was no smoke, and the main alarm was not activated, as it should have been.

A few days after our hearing about the latest Kent Lodge incident, the smoke alarm sounded in our own house in Dublin! It did not set off the main alarm and stopped after a minute or so. This happened on three occasions and was heard both by my wife and my daughter. We had the alarm people out, who patiently explained that we must have been mistaken, the smoke alarm box having been empty of all but a sensor and hence incapable of making any sound!

I hoped that these occurrences were not a consequence of my habit of trampling on graves!

[15]
Legal Documents

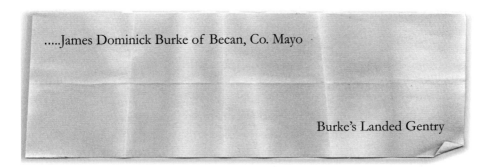

.....James Dominick Burke of Becan, Co. Mayo ·

Burke's Landed Gentry

To those not too excited about genealogical matters, it's doubtful if anything in the researcher's treasure chest looks less interesting than a copy of some very old deed or other legal document. These can be difficult to read, couched as they are not only in legal jargon but also in a form of English quite unfamiliar to the present generation. It takes time to adjust to the use of 'f' for 's', and to old hand writing, usually of excellent script, but sometimes not. However, invaluable information on property and people can be provided by such documents, and photocopies of originals have the additional benefit of showing actual signatures.

In the Registry of Deeds in Dublin I found two such documents that supported our knowledge of the Burkes of Becan. Although these provided reassurance rather than progress, giving credence to information already found, they were later to become of central importance in our search for the origins of James Dominick Burke. The first, and the oldest, was dated the 26th of November 1790,[45] and referred to a lease from Francis Burke of Bacon.

An indented deed of assignment made this 20th day of December 1789 Between Francis Burke of Becan in the County of Mayo Gent. of the one part and James Maxwell of the County of Galway Esq. of the other...the said Francis Burke hath granted sold transferred and made over unto the said James Maxwell the said Leases of the Tythes of the parishes of Becan Annagh Killollagh half Knock and also the Lease of Brackloon and the furniture of said house...

It was likely, but not certain, that this was Frank Burke of the Irish song who married Mary Kirwan on 12th May 1764 as described in the book on Becan.[31] His relationship to James Dominick was less obvious, however. Francis could have had a son in 1780, the approximate year of James Dominick's birth, but hardly a grandson. We also knew from the same book that Joseph Burke (of the Loughlin Cavalry) was living in 1796, and could have been a brother or an uncle of James Dominick. The deed, however, did refer to one 'Francis Burke of Bekan' and confirmed that he was living at Becan around the time of James Dominick's birth. Hopefully these details would help to put the pieces together when eventually we confirmed, as we hoped we would, the parentage of James Dominick.

The second document found was a marriage settlement registered nearly fifty years later on 31st December 1834, at 3.30 p.m.! This was the registration of a marriage settlement between 'John Francis Burke of Beacan' and 'Joseph Burke of Greenhill', Co. Mayo, which had been made on the 17th of November 1834.[46] Joseph Burke of Greenhill was the father of Anne Teresa Burke, who was marrying John Francis. We already knew John Francis to have been the Mayo County Coroner in 1840, so this was presumably the same man. Joseph was to give John Francis the sum of five hundred pounds along with his daughter, and John Francis was to put in trust for his wife the lands of Becan and Cloonfaghna. Most crucially of all for my interests, however, was that Francis Burke of Westport MD and Theobald Burke of Woodville were the trustees for John Francis. This confirmed the connection between the Hamilton Burke family of Westport and the Becan Burkes, although it did not tell us specifically what the relationship between the two families was.

Finding the marriage settlement raised the possibility that further relevant documents might have been registered. With this in mind I set about the task of carefully examining all of the appropriate Land and Name indexes there. Likely locations were checked including those that appeared on Deeds already found. For example, the 1790 Deed referred not only to Becan but also to Annagh, Killollagh and Knock. I searched the Names index under the various spellings of Burke, also Collingwood, Creagh and Collis and slowly but surely I found records of land transactions, marriage settlements and other legal transactions, all adding to our knowledge of these families.

The marriage of Louisa Jane and James Dominick, however, was still of critical importance, of that there was no doubt. Cousin Michael was continuing to search various records but without knowing where their marriage took place this was a daunting task. If we found the father of James Dominick, then we might well find the exact connection between the Becan Burkes and the Hamilton Burkes.

There could be a Hamilton Burke living to-day who holds the answer to most if not all of these questions, especially if his or her known pedigree went back as far as the days of Doctor Francis Burke of Westport. How might we find such a person? By advertising in genealogical circles? The telephone directory had no entries, but then perhaps the present generation used only the Burke surname, and there were too many of these to check. No Hamilton Burke pedigree was lodged with the Genealogical Office, so far as I could ascertain.

In searching for descendants of the Hamilton Burkes, the last reference found in the Connaught Telegraph was of a grandson of Francis and Margaret. I also discovered a death notice, in April 1951, of Captain John Hatton Noel Hamilton Burke, from Monkstown in Dublin, the son of 'Dr. and Mrs. Thomas Hamilton Burke'. He left a widow and no children.

One of the well-documented branches of Burkes were the Burkes of Ower, from whom we knew the Blake-Burkes were descended. In the Registry of Deeds, various documents found included names suggesting possible links between the Burkes from Becan and those from Ower. I found no concrete evidence, but I often came tantalisingly close! By checking all of the Burke records perhaps I would stumble across a lease or sale of land, or a marriage settlement or a Will, any of which could provide vital clues. It was simply a matter of persistence.

[16]
Unlikely Parentage

....Mr. John O'Mahony, a native of Ballybane, Firies.....

The Kerryman 1948

My mother seldom spoke of her family background, although I do recall mention of a constant stream of visitors to the family house in Glasnevin on the north side of Dublin. She was in her mid-thirties when she married and so, considering her extrovert nature, it was not surprising that there were many friends, both male and female, who would come to visit. Some of these visitors I understood to be cousins.

As my research of Collingwoods and Collises had brought me to the county of Kerry, I was provided with the opportunity to see what, if anything, I could discover of my mother's ancestry. Sharp contrasts existed between my mother's background and that of my father's, including farming communities undoubtedly of different religious and political persuasions to those on my father's side, which meant that my research would now be involved in areas so far unexplored.

My mother's father, John O'Mahony, came from Ballybane, from the farmhouse I had stumbled upon some twenty-five years previously!. He died when I was twelve years old and, although I remember him well, he never really talked to me and I knew nothing about his background. A rather sketchy tree was produced following discussions with family members. Despite continuing searches in the Tralee county library it remained rather inadequate compared with the Burke trees. The difficulty of compiling genealogical information on an Irish farming family became very apparent, and immediately betrayed a marked contrast between my mother's family and that of my father.

The 1901 census gave us some clues. It showed that the family were known as Mahony at that time. Why and when they dropped or acquired, the "O" is unknown. "Griffith's Valuation" showed that in the middle of the last century Cornelius Mahony had seventy-three acres at Ballybane, part of the Kenmare estate, in the parish of Molahiffe.[71]

We had always guessed that my mother's family had republican links, although as children we were unsure of what that meant. She often spoke of "friends" who visited her house in De Courcy Square, Glasnevin, before she married. It was only in later years that we realised that these included well-known republican figures such as Charlie Daly and Liam Lynch. My mother kept in memoriam cards in her prayer book with photographs with which we became familiar over the years. She had letters that were destroyed by my father after her death, for what reason I never really knew, although I have my suspicions. One of the most frustrating aspects of my research has been the thoughtlessness of members of the family in failing to keep material that would have been of such interest to others. It was particularly difficult to understand how my father of all people could have been guilty of a practice that he had himself criticised all his life.

It was only when I began the task of constructing an O'Mahony tree that I wondered if Charlie Daly was a cousin of my mothers. My great grandfather Cornelius had married one Ellen Daly from a nearby family (Fig.13). I remembered my mother showing me a book which had been published, in the nineteen-fifties I think, in which she was mentioned as having been at the Abbey Theatre with the late General Liam Lynch, Chief of Staff, I.R.A., shortly before his arrest. As a very young girl she lived at De Courcy Square in Glasnevin before moving to a larger house on Ballymun Road.

Charlie Daly became O.C. to the Second Northern Division of the I.R.A. He was an anti-Treatyite, and it came as a great shock to him to hear that it had been signed. Following the outbreak of the Civil War he was captured by Free State troops and imprisoned at Drumboe Castle in Co. Donegal. On March 14, 1923 he was executed with three comrades – Daniel Enright, Timothy O'Sullivan and Sean Larkin. The following extract was taken from a letter he wrote shortly before his execution that was reproduced in the book 'The Story of the Drumboe Martyrs'.[47]

I was very glad to get your letter this evening for although having heard from Father Brennan and Florrie O'Mahony that you and all at home had taken the news of my court-martial splendidly, I was still anxious…

Florrie O'Mahony was my mother, and clearly far more involved in politics than we had imagined as children. Among her belongings is a photograph of Charlie Daly seen talking to his brother, the last taken before his death.

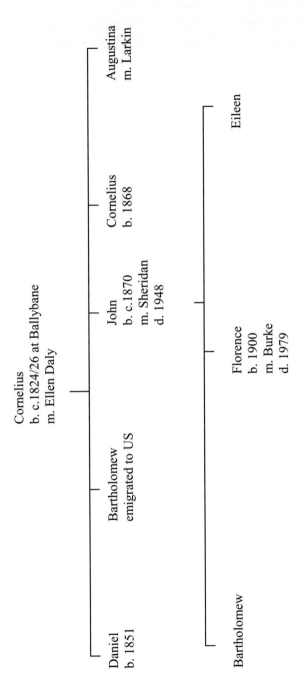

Fig. 13   *THE O'MAHONY FAMILY*

Cornelius
b. c.1824/26 at Ballybane
m. Ellen Daly

Daniel
b. 1851

Bartholomew
emigrated to US

John
b. c.1870
m. Sheridan
d. 1948

Cornelius
b. 1868

Augustina
m. Larkin

Bartholomew

Florence
b. 1900
m. Burke
d. 1979

Eileen

From this book, I learned that Charlie Daly had been arrested in my grandfather's home, 39 De Courcy Square, on New Year's Day 1921. At the time he was officially in charge of the organisation of the I.R.A. in Tyrone. By giving the name of a Kerryman who was living in Tyrone at the time, Daly was released, and in his frustration Major Mc Kennon proclaimed, *"That anybody sheltering Thomas McEllistrim, John Cronin, Maurice Carmothy and Charlie Daly would have their houses burned and themselves hanged by the neck"*.

A few hours after Daly's release, the British captured a letter that revealed his identity. Once again they raided 'O'Mahony's', but he was not there.

John O'Mahony was my grandfather and now I knew that my mother had grown up in a 'safe house'. Perhaps that was why my father had destroyed her letters after she had died. Indeed, when my grandfather died in 1948, the following obituary appeared in "The Kerryman":

It was with deep regret that the old people of Killarney and district learned of the death of Mr. John O'Mahony, a native of Ballybane, Firies. Living in Dublin for over sixty years, he never severed his ties with this district, having visited Killarney annually up to a few years ago. He had the honour of being a member of the first Kerry football team ever to play in Dublin and while in the capital, he identified himself with the National Movement and was a personal friend of the Irish Leaders, Arthur Griffith, Michael Collins and Eamonn de Valera. All Kerry Gaels knew him well and the late Dick Fitzgerald, Eugene O'Sullivan and Austin Stack were frequent visitors to his home. May he rest in peace.

I managed to make contact with a niece of Charlie Daly, who resided at the Daly house at Knockaneacoulteen, near Firies, and was in possession of the family papers which she had carefully preserved. I recognised the house from my mother's photographs, and spent some hours reading letters written by Charlie Daly and others. Included were several references to my grandfather, and letters that had been written to him throughout the civil war period. Clearly my grandfather was quite involved, and included in the papers was a telegram sent by him to inform Charlie Daly's mother of her son's execution.

Also included were two letters written by my mother in early 1923 following the execution of Charlie Daly and the killing of Liam Lynch, both of whom she had apparently known as good friends. It was a shock to recognise familiar handwriting in such a context, particularly as it was the first time I had ever seen a letter written by my mother as a young girl.

The relationship between the Dalys and O'Mahonys has not yet been established, although in her letters my mother had described herself as a cousin. It was interesting to realise that ancestors of both my parents, the Collingwoods and the O'Mahony's were living so close to each other at one time. Due to their very different backgrounds, they were unlikely ever to have met, although they may well have passed each other on the streets of Tralee!

Some time later in the National Library I found the book that my mother had shown me many years ago. It is called 'No Other Law', written by Florence O'Donoghue,[48] and described affairs that further related my grandparents' house to the republican movement.

The longest continuous period during which Liam [Lynch] remained in Dublin during the Tan War was after Christmas 1919. About 7th January he went there, [and there he] remained until 7th March. During these two months he was in frequent consultation with the officers of the GHQ Staff, particularly with Richard Mulcahy and Michael Collins. With Dan Breen and Sean Treacy he had many an animated discussion about plans for developing the fight. [...] While in Dublin, on this and on later occasions, Liam stayed at the house of Mr. and Mrs. John O'Mahony, De Courcy Square, where there was always a cordial welcome for him. Once during his first visit the house was raided during the daytime, but the raid did not appear to be especially for him. On another occasion when he was at the Abbey Theatre with Miss O'Mahony (now Mrs. Florence Burke), they met Sean Treacy there. As a result of a warning, all left before the performance had ended and they had only reached O'Connell Street when the Abbey was surrounded.

No Other Law

Despite this republican upbringing, my mother never displayed any anti-British sentiments and in fact spent the last twenty years of her life living in the vicinity of London, where she made many friends and spent some of the happiest years of her life. She was an extrovert who enjoyed the company of people, no matter where they came from. She died in her eightieth year, a good age that was in keeping with the tradition established by the other Burke wives who predeceased her. Louisa Jane was seventy when she died, Annie Goodwin seventy-five and my grandmother Annie Walshe, eighty-five (Fig.14). My own wife shows great interest in this statistic, despite the absence of a bloodline!

My father's characteristics and background could not have been more different. Of one thing he was certain. Despite our name we were of English Protestant stock, although he conceded that there was probably an Irish Clanricarde or whatever in the dim distant past. My father's father was English, as were his parents before him, but our generation were all born in Dublin and were Roman Catholics. Although

Fig.14 ***Annie Walsh***
My grandmother - a young widow who brought up a large family, played the
piano and spoke French.

I found out eventually how we came to be Irish, to this day I do not know what brought about the change of religion.

A strict disciplinarian, my father regarded those who drank a pint of Guinness as alcoholics. His particular interests were economics and philosophy, subjects unlikely to arise in normal conversation, and this probably accounted for his quiet disposition. Added to this, he cultivated a 'West-Brit' attitude,[49] not particularly endearing to his in-laws for reasons needing no explanation. A sense of balance was therefore achieved in the family by my mother's contrastingly extrovert character and Irish republican background. As children we never bothered to consider why our father might have preferred to have been born an Englishman, let alone a Protestant. It was only in later years, when aspects of family life in the previous generation were revealed that some of this began to make sense.

My father had a room – his 'study' – with a study chair and a study table. We children observed these from the door, as entry to the room was forbidden. Books and papers were everywhere. Small boxes could be seen, which we assumed contained wonders only fit for the eyes of adults. As children we accepted all of this because of "the diaries". My father kept a diary each day for almost sixty years, Browne & Nolan's Scribbling Diary with almanac, priced one shilling and sixpence in 1928. The diaries were in the study, and so we could understand why the room was off limits, diaries being particularly private, and hence mysterious.

After my father's death, it was with feelings of genuine guilt that I first dared to open these diaries. This emotion quickly turned to one of acute disappointment. Rather than a commentary on the political, economic and social environment of the time, all they contained were brief notes on the most mundane domestic matters. I had inherited a record covering over half a century of who had called to the house, what seeds were planted each spring, who was ill, who went where and what the weather was like!

Eventually I came to understand why he his confined comments to day-to-day activities. For one thing, he was able to check on dates of past family events which otherwise would have been forgotten. I am sure many can identify with the value of this strategy. One can read of the more important matters in the newspapers of the day, so why bother to repeat them in a personal diary. Nonetheless I was sorry that the diaries provided no insight into his thoughts and opinions.

My father's mother was Annie Walshe. We knew her as "little Granny", having been small of stature in comparison to our maternal grandmother. She died when I was young, in a household that consisted of one bachelor son and three unmarried daughters who thought the world of her. They lived on the north side of Dublin, and as children we needed no persuasion to visit our grandmother, uncle and aunts, which we did on many an occasion. Of course, they were only too happy to see their nephews. It was a comfortable home without rules and regulations for children and for my brothers and I these were very happy childhood times. We never failed to find a shilling, and sometimes a half-crown if a birthday was involved, in our pockets after we left.

"Little Granny" ruled the roost, yet she was a quiet, soft-spoken, gentle woman. She was well educated and had a particular love for music. Her family moved from Waterford to Dublin in her father's time. No doubt my father was aware that at the turn of the century the public house at numbers three and four Manor Street, Waterford, had eleven rooms occupied by the thirteen members of the family of William Walshe, the cousins of my grandmother.

She grew up in Chapelizod, and as a child played the piano with enough flair to be invited to people's houses to perform. It was on one of these occasions that she met Robert Herbert Burke, who was brought up in Colonel Brennan's substantial home, "The Grange" in Ballyfermot, with only some fields and the river Liffey separating it from Chapelizod. They married and had eight children. When the youngest was nine years old, Robert Herbert died of cancer. At the time, my father was serving aboard minesweepers in the First World War. He was the eldest of the children, and so returned home to help his widowed mother raise the children in very unfavourable financial circumstances. In later years we came to appreciate just how much affection and indeed respect he had for his mother.

The same feelings did not extend to Robert Herbert, his father, although at first I never really knew why. In his later years, my father talked in personal terms about his own family and he gave me the impression that he considered his father to have been irresponsible for having brought so many children into the world, and then left them for his widow to raise. I think that this also explained my father's disillusionment with the Catholic Church, particularly on the subject of birth control. This was in the early years of the twentieth century, when Protestant families were noticeably smaller than their Catholic counterparts.

Bearing in mind their characters, backgrounds and interests, how my parents ever married, let alone remained together, is something of a mystery to me, even to the present day. Nonetheless I have to admit that I grew up in a home that was warm and safe, and with parents who, despite their obvious differences, seemed remarkably compatible. I cannot recall a harsh word let alone an argument.

Another Accidental Discovery

> ....he (Francis Collingwood) married Ellen, second daughter of the late Rev. Samuel Collis, of Fort William in Co. Kerry in May 1822 by whom he had several children.....
>
> Naval Commanders

The Collingwoods remained the most likely source of information on the marriage of Louisa Jane into the Burke family. There were many branches of Collingwoods in England, some of whom had already provided much information by way of Collingwood family history, albeit nothing of note on the marriage in question. I felt certain the answer lay with a particular Collingwood and that all we needed to do was to track him or her down. How to accomplish this was another matter.

My original material on the Collingwood family was obtained from well-documented histories. After I acquired a more powerful computer I had the facility to correspond by e-mail with experienced researchers of Collingwoods in England. Of particular help were John and Brigit Sanders who provided me with substantial research material that must have taken them a lifetime to put together. From their records I was able to add further to our tree, although confining my entries to those connected with Louisa Jane.

One interesting lesson that I learned from my correspondence with the Sanders' was that some of my information was questionable, even that gleaned from respectable sources such as Burke's Landed Gentry. I realised that published pedigrees could not necessarily be taken at face value and that my own material might well be faulty. This is something the researcher has to live with and so I decided to continue with my system of assuming the information to be valid until such time as another source brought it into question.

The Sanders sent me details of many Collingwood lines going back to the seventeenth century. One line included an interesting character by the name of John Collingwood, supposedly from Eslington, who was married to a French girl in the Catholic Chapel of the Portuguese Embassy in London in 1731. They went to live in Bordeaux where they had a wine exporting business and later a vineyard. In 1751, John's daughter, Elizabeth, married Mark Kirwan from Galway. The pair inherited the vineyard where they built a small chateau which still exists and from which the very fine Margaux wine of Chateau Kirwan is produced to this day. We have on file a copy of what is said to be a portrait of Elizabeth, the daughter of John Collingwood. While I recorded this information purely for the sake of its anecdotal value, it later turned out to be of some significance. It was also relevant to another subject of which I am a fan – old Bordeaux wine!

Despite this wealth of information on the various Collingwood branches, it was surprising to me that no Irish line was included, bearing in mind that Francis Collingwood, who married Ellen Collis in 1822 and brought up his children near Tralee, was a well-known figure in his day. I was on my own when it came to searching for the ancestors of Francis and Ellen.

When I was in Tralee, from graveyard inscriptions and records given to me by the Church of Ireland office, I recorded details of individual Collingwoods but could not establish the relationships of one to another. I could find no living descendants and one particular entry in the Wills index[28] at the National Archives suggested that eventually only minor children remained and that these were probably returned to relations in England. There were no Collingwoods in the Irish telephone directories and none of my connections in the U.K. were aware of an Irish branch.

Mary O'Connor, who worked at the Tralee golf club, has written an excellent book about Barrow, Spa, Fenit and hinterlands, called *When Battle's Done*. She was of great help to me when I first visited Tralee by providing me with contacts and advice on potential sources of information. We were overheard one day chatting about the Collingwoods, and as a result I was given the name of a lady who lived in Tralee who was apparently related to a Collingwood. Eventually I found this lady, Sheila Kerins, who it turned out was the great-great granddaughter of Francis Collingwood and Ellen Collis.

Between us we were able to produce a family tree including the descendants of Francis and Ellen to the present day. Sheila is the last of the Irish Collingwoods. Her mother Hannah was the daughter of Francis Collingwood of Strand Street, grandson of Francis and Ellen Collis. He was probably the Collingwood "living in Tralee about one hundred years ago" of whom we had heard during our visit to Collingwood House.

I had the satisfaction of being able to send Sheila Kerins a print-out showing her family tree in Ireland over five generations, and of course her ancestry going back several hundred years. I was also able to tell her of a plaque on the wall of the church in Ashe Street, Tralee, in memory of Commander Francis Collingwood, erected by the Nelson Society. Sheila and I are fourth cousins.

This fortunate discovery led to another, which was in itself much more significant, although made in quite an accidental fashion. To ensure I had as much detail as possible, I called to the Registry of Deeds to carefully check the index for all Collingwood entries from 1822 onwards. This was not difficult. As I have already said, any Collingwood found was sure to be of the same family, and entries found were few and far between. I found various deeds that confirmed and added detail to the Collingwood record.

My system of recording previous searches then prompted me to check out a totally unrelated entry in the index. This involved land at Bacon[30] under the name of Kirwan. I had noted it on a previous visit but had not checked the Deed, as the Kirwan name was not then on my list of priorities. However in recent times I had been paying more and more attention to the Burkes of Ower and these we discovered had several connections with the Kirwans by marriage. Also, of course, the first traceable Burke of Becan was married to a Kirwan. Suddenly, by sheer chance, I found a definitive link between the Becan Burke and the Ower Burke families – the breakthrough we had been hoping for.

Memorial dated 6 Jan 1821 between George Aitken, late a Captain in H.M. South Cork Regiment of Militia and James Kirwan of Gardenfield Co Galway reciting that Mrs Mary Rogier by Indenture dated 9 July 1791 did grant to Mrs Mary Burke of Bacon Co Mayo, widow, lands 153 acres etc. to hold during lives of Charles Dillon, Henrietta Dillon and Charlotte Dillon, the children of Mary Rogier... and that the Rt. Hon. Thomas, Earl of Louth, by Indenture dated 15 October 1794 did grant to the said Mary Burke of Tuam Co. Galway, widow, land at Knochahalla, Knockavanny and Shavally Lusk commonly called Newtown Co. Galway to hold unto the said Mary Burke and William Lord Viscount Saint Laurence and of Francis Burke the son of the said Mary Burke...

This memorial of a deed went on to state that upon the death of Mary Burke, her land in Galway and Mayo was to be left to her daughters Mary Burke and Matilda Burke.[50] It also stated that Matilda Burke had gone on to marry George Aitken, who in turn assigned the land to James Kirwan. The deed had been witnessed by Denis Kirwan and Patrick Kirwan of Carnane.

I have already referred to the potential value of old deeds and documents. Included here was evidence that Mary Burke of Bacon was a widow with at least three children – a son Francis and two daughters Mary and Matilda.

I then found an Indenture dated 9 July 1791 which showed that in the previous year the Right Honourable Charles Lord Viscount Dillon and Mrs Mary Rogier had granted the lands of Becan to the children of Mary Rogier, Charles, aged 14, Henrietta aged 9 and Charlotte aged 6.[51]

An unconnected 1938 marriage settlement proved relevant because of the parties involved.[52] These included John Burke of Ower, James Kirwan of Castletown, Co. Galway, Patrick Kirwan of Carnane, Walter Burke of Queensfort, Co. Galway, John and Ellen Kirwan of Galway and their children James, Catherine and Maria.

The various names and connections were confusing, to say the least! However these three documents led to one important conclusion. Patrick Kirwan of Carnane and John Burke of Ower were almost certainly related by marriage, as both were parties to the 1838 marriage settlement. We already knew of an Ower and Kirwan relationship from our Blake-Burke tree and other published records, but now we had a document that included the same Patrick Kirwan of Carnane and Mary Burke of Becan. For the first time the three families of Kirwans, Burkes of Becan and Burkes of Ower were tied together.

It was clear that Viscount Dillon, who owned the Burke land at Becan, was the grandfather of Charles, Henrietta and Charlotte. His son had probably died and the son's widow Mary married again to one Rogier. This was eventually confirmed from the Dillon records.

What was much more curious was discovering that Mary Burke was a widow in 1791, still residing at Becan, but by 1794 had moved to Tuam. One quite reasonable explanation for this would have been that Mary Burke had moved back to her original family home, which meant she was Mary Kirwan before her marriage. This theory would also explain the other Kirwan names on the deeds.

This was just a guess of course, until I remembered Nollaig Ó Muraile's reference to the marriage of Frank Burke. Frank, "with his bright flawless cheeks and shining blue eyes" was married on the 12th of May 1764, at Tuam, to Miss Mary Kirwan, daughter of Richard Kirwan of the Co. Galway, Esq.

The more I thought about it the more I became convinced that I had found the Mary Kirwan who married Francis Burke of Becan. According to the deed she had one son, possibly her eldest, Francis, who must have been left to manage the farm on the Spotfield estate at Becan.

It was important to search for clues leading to the positive identification of the characters involved. The younger Francis, mentioned in the later deed, obviously had his father's name. Assuming the parents were aged about twenty years in 1764, the year of their marriage, this would make Francis Senior less than fifty years of age when he died, his death probably causing the deed to be executed. It all fitted in so neatly - names, dates and locations.

Then the penny dropped! If Mary Burke of Becan was the wife of Frank Burke of the old song, and if there was only one prominent Burke family in Becan, where did James Dominick fit in? The answer was obvious. James Dominick had to be one of the children of Francis Burke and Mary Kirwan.

It all made sense. Consider the family situation now emerging from the records. The 1791 deed referred to a son, Francis, possibly named after his father. Presumably he was the eldest and inherited the farm. His mother Mary would probably have been in her late thirties in 1780 when James Dominick was born. Indeed James Dominick could have been the youngest in the family. The Burkes of the Becan Planxty were "minor landed gentry" and so of course they could afford to send James Dominick to college in Dublin.

By now I had established contact with a number of experienced genealogists who assured me there would only have been one Burke family occupying the Spotfield Estate in Becan whose son's marriage notice would have appeared in Pue's Occurrences. In fact they went much further and suggested that, taking the dates into account, it was unreasonable to assume anything other than that James Dominick was the son of Francis Burke and Mary Kirwan. Either parent could have died before 1780, but the deeds I had found proved that Francis probably died not long before 1790 and that the widow Mary Burke of Becan had returned to Tuam by 1794.

The experts regarded the findings as conclusive. I was reminded that no further proof may exist, and that from a genealogical point of view I had made the connection.

However despite these reassurances a doubt lingered in my mind. I could still think of other explanations, however unlikely. I hastily went back over all my records. The earliest record of a Burke in Becan was the Will of Thomas Burke in 1757. Almost certainly he would have to have been Frank Burke's father.

[18]
The Kirwans of Galway

At this point a whole new avenue of exploration had been opened – the Kirwans of Galway. If I was right, Mary Kirwan was my third great grandmother and I had Kirwan blood in my veins. More cousins! Kirwan genealogy should be easily found and this might give me the proof I needed to establish beyond doubt the relationship between our two families, indeed three families when the Burkes of Ower were included. The main focus at this point was on the relationship of Thomas Burke to Francis Burke. Yet again I was setting off on the trail of a Burke wife, hopefully to lead to another successful conclusion.

The Kirwans were one of the Galway Tribes.[53] William Kirwan settled in the town of Galway in 1488 and died there in 1499. From him and his brother, it is said, are descended all the Kirwan families of Galway and Mayo. The good news was that these were reasonably well researched – the bad news was there were many branches, all including Richards, Martins, Patricks, Johns and so on. The main branches were situated at Blindwell, Castlehacket, Cregg, Gardenfield, Glan, Hillsbrook, and Woodfield in the county of Galway, and Dalgin in the county of Mayo.

I had come to one of those points which demanded some serious detective work. I knew that the Mary Kirwan who married Frank Burke was a daughter of Richard Kirwan, the marriage having taken place at Tuam. However, most of the Galway Kirwan estates were located around the Tuam area, and she could have come from any one of these.

On the shelves of the Royal Irish Academy in Dublin is a Kirwan Pedigree compiled from originals.[54] This mentioned other publications containing Kirwan material and included separate trees for the Cregg, Woodfield, Hillsbrook and Dalgan branches, amongst others. I carefully took note of these and fed them into the computer, at the same time noting with growing unease the proliferation of Richard Kirwans. As usual those unenlightened genealogists in the past omitted to pay any attention to the women of the family and failed to record their names, referring to them as mere 'daughters'. I found this extremely frustrating, not only because it made my search for Mary Kirwan more difficult, but also because of the chauvinism expressed by it. I later discovered, to my great surprise, that this particular brand of chauvinism is alive and well among genealogists to this very day!

I eventually came across a reference to a Francis Burke who was the son-in-law of Richard Kirwan of Gardenfield in Co. Galway. This Richard Kirwan had died in 1820, so the dates were not out of line.

In the Genealogical Office there is a box containing the most extraordinary letters,[55] diaries and records relating to the Kirwan family. These provide a vivid picture of events, gossip and life over a number of years in the last century. No doubt serious researchers of the Kirwan family know all about them, but to me they were a revelation and an example of fascinating material preserved in the archives. As well as providing an invaluable guide to who was who, parts were little short of hilarious.

Letter 7th July 1840 from Edmond Kirwan, 15 Hardwick Street, Dublin:

In 1850 in Liverpool I told my darling lovely wife to have my dinner ready at 6 o'clock. I went on to a passenger ship to see a relation of mine that was going to New Orleans. I missed to get out in the Tugg Boate or Pilot Boate and I was brought to New Orleans. Obliged to write to my wife from America to send me money to bring me home…

This record of the personal details made a welcome break from the cold statistics that I was used to working with. My search for my ancestor Richard Kirwan led to the discovery of an account of his namesake, the famous scientist.[56]

Richard Kirwin of Menlo Castle, Galway, was not only the greatest scholar, but the greatest oddity of his time. He attended Vice-regal levees wearing a large slouched hat which he never removed; he received his friends, summer and winter, lying on a couch in front of a blazing fire; he kept a pet eagle and six Irish wolfhounds; his diet consisted entirely of ham and milk. Kirwin died following an attempt to "starve" a cold on 1ˢᵗ June 1812 in his 79ᵗʰ year and was buried in St. George's Church, Temple Street, Dublin.

Naturally I began to wonder if the eccentricities within my own family were inherited from my third great grandmother of whose existence I was unaware until now! There were other Kirwan reports of a more serious nature. For example, I read the Proceedings in the case of the Crown against William Burke Kirwan for the murder of his wife on Ireland's Eye on 6ᵗʰ September 1852.[57]

During the course of researching and building a substantial record of the Kirwan family, I discovered the connection between the Kirwans of Hillsbrook and the Burkes of Ower which appeared on the Blake-Burke tree which my father and I had traced from Colwyn Bay many years previously. This raised the thought that Uncle Tom may have known about a Kirwan connection, although to my knowledge no relationship existed between the Hillsbrook Kirwans and our own family.

I was able to add the Blake-Burke details, descendants of the Burkes of Ower, to my Kirwan tree. There were now in effect two family histories and the objective was to connect the two if possible. It was tempting to add Frank Burke and Mary Kirwan as the parents of James Dominick, but I was still hesitant, despite the evidence we had uncovered. I needed to be certain that there was no possibility of James Dominick belonging to another family of Burkes from Becan.

I wondered if anything more could be found regarding the Richard Kirwan of Gardenfield whose daughter had married a Burke. Returning to the Registry of Deeds, I carried out a long and tedious examination of every deed recorded in the index in the name of Richard Kirwan commencing in 1730. Perseverance paid off. On the 20ᵗʰ November 1771 a land transaction was recorded between 'Richard Kirwan of Gardenfield, Co. Galway and Francis Burke of Bacon, Co. Mayo'.[58] This was quite a discovery as not only did it prove that a Francis Burke of Becan was living in 1771, seven years after the marriage of Frank and Mary, but it was strong evidence that Mary was of the Gardenfield branch.

I ordered copies of the Francis Burke of Becan deed of 1789 and this 1771 deed in order to compare signatures. Disappointingly the signatures on each document appeared to be different. However, one explanation could have been that the deeds were executed by a father and a son of the same name. This, if true, would have meant that Francis Burke senior died in or before 1789.

The Gardenfield transaction could still have been coincidental however, and in any case my Gardenfield pedigree showed that Richard Kirwan's daughter, Elizabeth, and not Mary, had married a Francis Burke. However, I already knew of other details in this particular tree that were incorrect. Perhaps the daughter's name was Mary Elizabeth - this would account for James Dominick's eldest child being named Maria Eliza. Was this wishful thinking? On re-checking Maria's probate record found in the National Archives I discovered it was indeed registered in the name of Maria Elizabeth. The plot was thickening.

The final proof was not long in coming. The marriage notice in Pue's Occurrences that had been recorded by Nolliag Ó Muraile referred to Mary, daughter of Richard Kirwan of the County Galway. I enquired from the Gilbert Library in Dublin if any other 1764 newspapers were preserved and could be scrutinised.[59] I was told that the Freeman's Journal was the only one covering that date and copies were available on microfilm. This was a national newspaper printed twice weekly. It contained virtually no births other than royalty and very few marriages and deaths. Considering the entire population of Ireland at the time the chances of Francis Burke and Mary Kirwan appearing were remote – but there they were, in the edition covering 12th to 15th May 1764.

Mr. Francis Burke of Becane in the County of Mayo to Mifs Mary Kirwan, daughter of Richard Kirwan of Cahianegarinty in the County of Galway, Efq.

Gardenfield was the Anglisised version of Cahianegarinty which fortunately was included in the Freeman's Journal notice!

Mary Kirwan was my third great grandmother and the predecessor of Louisa Jane Collingwood, Annie Goodwin, and Annie Walshe as Burke wives.

Whereas I had been fortunate to learn so much about the personal lives of Louisa Jane and both Annies, I had to accept as unlikely that any record remained which might tell us about the Mary Kirwan who married a man with "shining blue eyes" in 1764. It was such a long time ago.

I was reminded of Michael Coady's lines:[60]

> *A life I'll never know*
> *Is buried with you*
> *In a place I'll never find*

[19]

Aristocracy

This could have been the end of the search, or at least an appropriate finish to
the story. After all it's not every day that one discovers the identity of a great-
grandmother who lived in the eighteenth century. A reasonably neat and tidy
conclusion, I thought. And so I made the decision to wrap things up and my
colleagues in genealogical circles were informed of the great event.

However, having learned that Mary Kirwan was my third great grandmother, it
seemed reasonable to research her Kirwan ancestors. The Kirwans could be added
to the tree, joining the Collingwoods and Goodwins who had followed them in
marrying into the Burke family. The Kirwan tree traced their family details back
to Martin Kirwan who died in 1691 and his son, Richard, who married Margaret
Browne in 1673.[61]

I realised how fortunate it was that my genealogy computer programme was up and
running. Trying to keep track of my findings with hand-written notes at this stage
would have been quite impossible. I was amazed to learn that I now had almost
two thousand names in the programme, all blood relations or related by marriage.

A print-out of the tree collated to date showed up at least one disappointing feature.
We all have thirty-two third great grandparents – so far I had identified only ten!
Despite my inclination to follow female lines, the results suggested there may have
been too much concentration on Burke families. The Gormans, Caines, Wards and

Higgins were all ancestors of Annie Walshe, most of that information coming from her diary. More significantly, with the Becan revelations I had come to the end of the line of Burkes in the eighteenth century, whereas for example the Collingwoods included Cuthbert, my ninth great grandfather, born in 1566.

Having learned the value of investigating the ancestry of those ladies who married into the principal families of the search, and knowing that any number of new discoveries can be made in following up these routes, I applied this idea to the Kirwan branch. I discovered that Mary Kirwan's mother was Honora Bermingham of the family of the Barons of Athenry. Aristocracy at last! A copy of her marriage certificate dated 3rd August 1737 described Honora as the daughter of John Bermingham of Dalgin, grandson of Edmund, Lord Athenry.[62] This was a real breakthrough as detailed records of the now extinct Athenry peerage could be quite interesting.

The significance of this quickly became apparent. The Athenry lineage was readily available,[63] reaching back to the twelfth century in Ireland. Researching the Barony of Athenry pedigree revealed not only my Bermingham ancestors, but also, through their marriages, maternal blood links and connections with other distinguished families.

Without too much difficulty I traced each generation of Berminghams from Honora's marriage to Richard Kirwan in 1734 back to Robert de Bermingham who lived in the twelfth century – seventeen generations in all. To have traced my ancestry back to Robert de Bermingham, my twentieth great-grandfather, was the greatest achievement of my search so far, and yet again this breakthrough had come from following the female line.

The Bermingham family takes their surname from the old castle of Bermingham in the county of Warwick, the locality in which the city of Birmingham is now situated. Peter or Piers de Bermingham held the castle. In 1172, Robert de Bermingham accompanied Strongbow to Ireland following which his son, Peter, was the first Bermingham to take possession of the lands at Athenry. Some sources regard him as the first Lord Athenry and although there is disagreement regarding his date of death, it is thought to have been sometime between 1252 and 1270. However it was his son, Meyler, who built Athenry Abbey for the Dominican friars in 1241. Meyler died in 1263 and was buried in Athenry Abbey. This was to become the burial place of many of his successors. His younger son, William, was appointed Archbishop of Tuam in May 1289.

Interestingly, when tracing the family of my grandmother Annie Walshe, I had learned of the origins of Walshes in this country. The 'Le Waleys' had accompanied

Robert Fitzstephen, a cohort of Strongbow, to Ireland as part of the twelfth century invasions. I wondered if the Walshes and Berminghams had known each other!

A visit to Galway spent locating old Kirwan estates around the Tuam area, including those at Gardenfield, Castlehacket and Carnane, led to Athenry and the remains of the castle and the Dominican Friary built by my seventeenth grand-uncle, Meyler de Bermingham, the second Lord Athenry. I was still having difficulty coming to terms with the aristocratic links. Whereas I felt I had developed some affinity with Louisa Jane Collingwood, this was more difficult to achieve with those who lived in the thirteenth century. Reference to 'old uncle Meyler' seemed a bit over the top!

I could not resist the temptation to employ the mathematical skills of my computer to calculate just how many twentieth great grandparents each of us have. The answer was a rather disconcerting four million, one hundred and ninety-four thousand, three hundred and four. I had found one, so far!

It had taken me many years to find my third great-grandparents in Becan and now, within a relatively short space of time, I had discovered another seventeen generations. It was ironic to think of all the effort it had taken to get to this point – travelling around the country, meeting people, looking at castles, graveyards and haunted houses. Because I had now traced ancestors married into well-recorded families, the research had become focused on the recorded pedigrees of those families. Things had changed!

Had other researchers in recent times managed to connect the families of the landed gentry together and produce one pedigree showing precisely the relationships one to the other? This is precisely what I was now constructing, each entry linked through marriage to my Burke family. It seemed that I had taken a significant step from being a well-meaning amateur to being someone with quite a serious academic project on his hands.

Marriages between Burkes, Bourkes, Brownes, Berminghams, Blakes, Dalys, D'Arcys, Kirwans and others were faithfully recorded, although the handing down of forenames made it extremely difficult on occasions to determine exactly who was who within each family. I maintained the discipline of restricting new information to those connected by marriage to families already on the tree. An increase to almost four thousand entries was an indication of the work involved, the information coming from a wide variety of sources. Although my movements had become static in the sense that I was no longer rushing around the countryside, the research had reached an absorbing level of intensity.

My investigation into the Blake family yielded equally impressive results. In 1278, the castle and lands of Kiltorroge in county Galway were granted to one Richard Caddel, who took the name of Niger (Black) or Blake, and was the common ancestor of all the Blake families in Connaught. I researched the Blakes descended from Richard Caddel and recorded the pedigrees of many branches, including the Blakes of Menlough who appeared on my Blake-Burke tree.

One family member of particular noteworthiness was Joseph Henry Blake, the third Baron Wallscourt of Ardfry who was born in 1797 and died in Paris of cholera in 1849.[64] Among his eccentricities were a tendency to become violent, being of great physical strength and renowned skill in boxing, and of a little more offbeat nature, the habit of walking around his house with no clothes on, carrying a cow-bell to warn the maid servants of his approach!

This research led me eventually to those in the family who appeared on the Blake-Burke tree. This was quite an achievement after so many years, although it was still frustrating not to know precisely what Father Tom Burke saw in the tree which led him to recognise his line. It seemed highly unlikely that he could have been aware of the connections I was now establishing, going back to the eighteenth century. However there were more recent marriages, any one of which may have provided him with the necessary clue.

Having noted the marriage of Joseph Henry Blake, the first Lord Wallscourt, to Louisa Catherine Bermingham, daughter of Thomas, Lord Athenry, I discovered that Louisa Catherine had a sister, Mary, who married William St. Lawrence, the second Earl of Howth, in 1777. I then spotted a newspaper article referring to a "fashionable marriage" in 1894 at the Church of St. Francis Xavier, Gardiner Street, Dublin.[65] The marriage was between Stephen St. Lawrence Bourke and Maria Blake-Burke, eldest daughter of Major Walter Blake-Burke. It did not take long to figure out that the bride was a sister of Sammy Blake-Burke who lived in Colwyn Bay, whose grave my father and I had found in north Wales, and in whose house Father Tom had seen the family tree.

[20]
Granuaile

Ultimately I did accomplish my quest to trace my ancient Burke ancestors – but ironically, yet again it was not through the male line.

The maritime connections had continued down through the generations of my family to my father who served in the Royal navy during World War One. Along the way we had Louisa Jane Collingwood of the well-known naval family that included her grandfather, Edward, who accompanied Anson on the first ever circumnavigation of the world in the eighteenth century. Her illustrious cousin, Admiral Cuthbert, took over the fleet and was victorious at Trafalgar, and her brother Francis shot and killed the Frenchman who mortally wounded Nelson. James Dominick was a surgeon aboard ships. An impressive seafaring lot!

Little did I know that an even more impressive maritime character was about to emerge, and a member of the Burke family at that!

The lengthy Bermingham pedigree showed a number of marriages to Burkes and Bourkes throughout the centuries that I hoped would lead eventually to my particular Burke ancestors. However, following my recently established routine, I decided first of all to investigate Honora Bermingham's mother. She was Elizabeth Browne, daughter of Colonel John Browne who was one of the parties to the Treaty of Limerick in 1691, was the ancestor of the Earls of Altamont, and had built the first Westport House in the latter part of the seventeenth century. Colonel Browne's father was Sir John Browne, first Baronet of The Neale.

The final twist came when I discovered the name of the wife of Colonel Browne, Elizabeth's mother. She was Maude Bourke, daughter of the third Viscount Bourke of Mayo. She was my seventh great-grandmother and her portrait hangs in the main hall of Westport House. I met the present Lord Altamont who kindly arranged a private viewing of Westport House, including the portrait. He seemed less than excited to hear that we were seventh cousins, once removed, but did provide me with a fascinating account of the history of Westport House, built by Maude and her husband.

John Browne, an Englishman, settled at the Neale in county Mayo about 1580. He assisted Sir John Perrott and Sir Richard Bingham in carrying out the composition of Mayo in 1585, whereby the chieftains and freeholders of Mayo acknowledged the sovereignty of Queen Elizabeth and agreed to adopt English laws and tenures. In 1583 he was appointed the first sheriff of the newly created county of Mayo. In 1589, while serving the office of Sheriff for the second time, he was slain by the Bourkes of Mayo who were then in insurrection. This John Browne was the great-grandfather of Colonel Browne, husband of my sixth great grandmother Maude Bourke, whose descendants now reside at Wesport House in the county of Mayo.

I was now back to Bourkes, albeit spelt with an "o", and research into Maude's family would at last bring me to the origins of the Burkes in Ireland. Little did I suspect when I started out that I would ever reach this point, let alone do so by following the history of my great-grandmothers rather than their Burke husbands.

The lineage of Maude Bourke and the Viscount Mayo line provided an unexpected revelation. Maude was the great-great granddaughter of Grace O'Malley, the famous Granuaile, Sea Queen of the West, whose husband was Sir Richard "an Iarainn" Bourke. Carrying on the tradition of remarkable women in the family, Granuaile took her place in the family tree as my tenth great grandmother!

Much has been written about Grace, daughter of Owen O'Malley and married originally to O'Flaherty, chief of West Connaught. Grace inherited a small fleet from her father, took command and became well known for many bold expeditions from her stronghold on Clare Island off the coast of Mayo. After her second marriage to Richard Bourke, she set sail for London about 1575 where she was received at the court of Queen Elizabeth. There appeared to be a mutual respect between the two women and, although refusing any honours herself, Grace was happy to see her son Theobald, called Tibbot na Long, or 'Theobald of the Ships' because he was born at sea, knighted. Charles I subsequently created him Viscount Mayo. Tibbot was the great grandfather of Maude Bourke.

There is a well-known story about Granuaile who, was so aggrieved when she was unwittingly refused hospitality on one occasion at Howth Castle, took the rather drastic step of kidnapping one of the children. The child was returned eventually upon receiving an assurance that a place would be set for the Sea Queen at dinner each evening just in case she should call again. The ritual continues to the present day. It occurred to me that perhaps her tenth great-grandson could avail of a free meal should he fall on hard times. I had a brief word with the present owner who was unimpressed!

William, the progenitor of the Burkes in Ireland, was my *twentieth* great grandfather, and my record now showed the names of each of his descendants down to one of the most recent additions to the family, our latest granddaughter Kate Burke. Hopefully I will still be around when she is old enough to appreciate the exploits of Granuaile and other extraordinary forebears, many of whom were women. I was particularly pleased to find Granuaile whom I regarded not only as the first real heroine on our family tree but also the original seafaring member.

Having added Kirwans, Berminghams and Brownes, the direct ancestral record had now extended to my fourteenth great grandparents. Connected to my direct line were families such as Butlers, Fitzgerald and O'Malleys, together with peerage and landed gentry over several generations.

With unseemly haste entire pedigrees were added and the number of entries in my computer record grew, and grew![72] My hobby had become a project of some genealogical significance, having commenced in such a modest fashion with my father so many years ago. He would have found it hard to believe, let alone accept, such an illustrious ancestry. I suppose to the landed gentry it is not unusual to have this kind of record, but to someone like myself, coming from quite an ordinary background, it seemed odd to say the least.

I became familiar with the pedigrees of many distinguished families living in Ireland throughout the centuries. It was reasonable to include blood relations on the tree, but to branch off into relations through marriage was no longer a feasible proposition if I was to retain my sanity. I would peruse published lineages, searching for familiar names, particularly those of female members, concentrating on families resident in the west of Ireland. In this way I discovered connections not evident from the published records. Admittedly I did succumb occasionally to researching branches that looked no more than interesting, being unable to resist the possibility of a link to some historical character or indeed to some well-known figure of the present day.

Following this routine led to a multiplicity of connections between well-known and not-so-well-known families, and I realised at that point that I was building a unique record. Browsing through editions of 'Burke's Landed Gentry' in the hope of finding yet another obscure connection became addictive. Before long there were over eight thousand entries on the tree.

Covering nineteen generations, the record now included Walter Butler, Earl of Ormonde, Donagh O'Brien, Earl of Thomond, Gerald Fitzgerald, Earl of Kildare, and James Fitzgerald, Earl of Desmond in addition to rather distinguished D'Arcys, Fitzmaurices, de Lacys and Barrys.

The historians assert that all Burkes are related to the original William, so that all Burkes and Bourkes shared the same ancestry. However I understood now that the real achievement of my work was not just in confirming this, but in being able to name each individual family member from those ancient times to the present day.

Because the pedigrees of these families were so well documented, I now had at last an ancestry that reached as far back as Charlemagne, and which included innumerable cousins through marriages into other members of the landed gentry.

Fig. 15   THE BURKES OF BEKAN

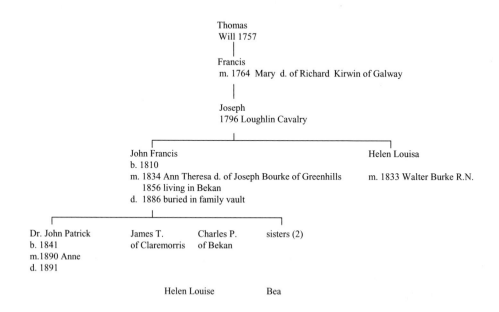

[21]
The Burkes of Becan

Tracing my Burke ancestry to Becan was a real achievement and somehow or other, despite the involvement of more illustrious families, I knew that when it came to break off and write the story of my search, it should finish with these Burkes (Fig.15).

Almost certainly the Spotfield estate and the lands at Becan were given to a son of one of the well-established Burke branches, perhaps a younger son who did not inherit the title of his father. The Becan book described the Burkes as minor catholic gentry, so presumably the lineage was well known at the time. The family was wealthy.

Was the Thomas Burke of Becan, whose will was dated 1757, the father of Frank?

So far I had failed to locate the ancestors of Frank Burke of Becan. Wills have always been a potential source of information on the wealthy classes, particularly if dated post-1857. However, researching wills and administration bonds before then can be a frustrating exercise. After 1857 the Public Record Office[11] held the responsibility for preserving probate records and these can now be viewed on shelves in the National Archives. Although virtually all original wills and administrations were destroyed in the PRO fire of 1922, the Vicar's Index[38] included reference to Thomas Burke of Becan in 1757. On enquiry I was told that no further evidence of this would be found. Subsequently I became aware that certain estates of over £5 were, in certain circumstances, the responsibility of the

Prerogative Court under the authority of the Archbishop of Armagh and it was these that were covered in Vicar's index.

One day, whilst browsing through potential sources of material on the Bingham family (by now I knew that Charles Bingham, the first Lord Lucan, was my twentieth cousin!), I decided to check the Abstracts of Wills recorded by Sir William Betham, then Deputy Ulster King of Arms, in the early part of the last century. These were on microfilm at the National Library and were hand-written extracts from wills that Betham made during his term of office showing the relationship between family members. The records were in alphabetical order and so 'Bingham' and 'Burke' were together on the same reel of film. I turned to the Burke and Bourke entries and then remembered I had perused these on a previous occasion without success, due mainly to the illegibility of many entries. I asked and was given permission to examine the originals in the Manuscripts Reading Room.

The originals were quite clear. There were many Burke and Bourke extracts, all with a short pedigree showing other family members. Included was 'Thomas Bourke of Bacon in County Mayo' whose will was dated 10th March 1756! The entry recorded that his wife was Mary and that he had one son Francis and three daughters. Examination of all the Burke wills recorded by Betham before 1756 showed none from Becan. This strongly suggested that Thomas was the original occupier of the Spotfield estate and that Frank of the 'shining blue eyes' was his son.

The Becan book had included reference to a Tom Burke advertising the sale of land in the Becan area in 1752 and this now fell neatly into place. In some ways I felt that this discovery should have been made earlier, that I could have been more attentive to the potential of recorded wills which were available.

A further check on those who had died without having made a will in "All the Administrations to Intestates in the Prerogative Office in Dublin from the earliest time to 1802" revealed that one Frank Burke of Bacon had died intestate. The bond was dated the 29th May 1789 and the administrators appointed were his daughter Mary and his widow Mary. The date of death confirmed my theory, worked out from the various deeds discovered earlier, that the same Francis Burke had died shortly before December 1789. Names and dates fitted neatly into place. After all this time, another generation of the Becan Burkes had been found.

But who were the ancestors of Thomas Burke of Becan?

The involvement of members of the Burkes of Ower in later deeds suggests that this was the family of Thomas. Ulick Burke of Ower was the son and heir in the seventeenth century, and he had two brothers named Thomas and Francis. Filling the gap between them and the birth of Thomas Burke of Becan might well complete the direct male line between the original William de Burgo and myself. As I write, this connection has not been made but I am confident it is only a matter of time. It would have provided an appropriate ending to the story - but then who wants this to finish?

*Fig.16 **Barretstown Castle***
An ancestral estate, now home to the Paul Newman Gang Camp

[22]

Barretstown and other Castles

John, the eight and last Viscount Mayo, died in 1767 since when the title has lain dormant......

Lodge's Peerage of Ireland

I could not resist the temptation to follow-up some of the more interesting connections revealed in the ancient Burke pedigree. When I saw the Creagh pedigree for the first time, descending from William the Conqueror, I regarded it as a most remarkable piece of research, and certainly had no expectation of emulating it myself. Yet that is what I had achieved. William de Burgo had accompanied William the Conqueror to England in 1066, and we had now found direct descendants of each, Emma Burke and Michael Creagh, who had married almost eight hundred years later.

A connection with the British Royal family arose from the marriage of Ellen de Burgh and Robert de Bruce. A daughter, Marjorie had a son, Robert the Steward, who was born in 1316, became King of Scotland and was the first of the Stuarts. Their descendants can be found in the history books but it was with a feeling of unreality that I added them to the family tree. It was necessary to remind myself that every Burke in Ireland was similarly related, although again I wondered how many knew it, let alone could trace each link in the chain.

I was interested to find out which of the Royals were of the same generation as myself. The answer included Queen Victoria, who was my twentieth cousin. I was reluctantly forced to accept that this newly found fame was probably of little benefit in any material way. People were unlikely to bow when I entered the room and I was fairly sure an inheritance was out of the question - even the computer was unable to calculate how many twentieth cousins of Victoria existed, but one could safely assume there were millions.

William de Burgh, the progenitor of the Irish Burkes, was a descendant of Robert de Burgh who fought at the battle of Hastings and is depicted on the Bayeaux Tapestry. The Blake-Burke pedigree that I copied from the original many years ago commenced with Pepin who died in the year 768, through Charlemagne who died in 814 and down to this Robert de Burgh, the descendent of William. Early historical records confirm the descendancy of the de Burghs from Charlemagne .

William de Burgh was a brother of Hubert de Burgh, the second most powerful man in England, next to the King, who helped draft the Magna Carta at Runnymede in 1215. William came to Ireland around 1185, having been given large tracts of land by King John. He married firstly Elizabeth, daughter of King Edward I of England, by whom he had a son, Richard Mor, and secondly the daughter of Daniel Mor O'Brien, last King of Cashel. Daniel was the grandson of Brian Boru.

Richard Mor de Burgh became Lord of Connaught and founded the town of Galway about 1232. He was Lord Lieutenant of Ireland in 1227 and died in 1243. His brother Richard Og was the ancestor of the Burkes of Clanricarde. One of Richard's children, Walter, became the first Earl of Ulster and it was his great-great granddaughter, Elizabeth, who in 1352 married Lionel, Duke of Clarence, and thus consolidated the de Burgh link with the English royal family.

The many lines of descendants of Charlemagne included the Viscounts Mayo, the first of whom was Granuaile's son. The title lay dormant following the death of the eighth Viscount although many believed it should have passed to one David Bourke. a direct descendant of Granuaile. His family came from the Ballyhaunis area. One wonders ....!

It would have been all too easy to get carried away with the emergence of such impressive ancestors, but not all historians regarded the Burkes with admiration. In J.F.Quinn's *History of Mayo*,[66] the Burkes were depicted far from favourably.

Long before the 13th century British domination had cursed Ireland, and the Burkes were not a native family. Originally de Burgo, they came across the water and were called Normans, afterwards being known as Anglo-Normans, and through their activities the whole country was put under the heel of England. They were actually Englishmen who married into Irish families, and when they had themselves well entrenched they tried to beat off the British, failed and were they themselves submerged, bringing ruination to the entire country.

The computer programme grew rapidly, enabling me to add more and more connected entries. Of course the question was where or when to stop. Marriages between landed gentry families were commonplace and one could go on forever adding to the tree.

I was also aware of perhaps too great a concentration with the past and not enough curiosity about the descendants of these prominent families. Which were the lines that survived and which became extinct along the way? Until now the discovery of long lost cousins, travelling and meeting people from all parts of the country had breathed life into what could easily have become an academic exercise, a dull and rather uninteresting hobby. For this reason I decided to take a more active interest in the houses still standing which at one time were the residences of these distinguished families. In some cases what I discovered about present day occupancy was interesting, to say the least.

Some buildings had disappeared altogether, others were in various states of delapidation, but many had been maintained and restored over the centuries. Mention has already been made of visits to Howth Castle and Westport House, but recent additions to the tree meant the list could now be substantially extended. Initially I had confined my interest to residences of more "recent" blood relations, houses such as Kent Lodge, Ardraw House, Little Mount Pleasant, Collingwood House, Fort William and of course Becan House. But the discovery of even more notable ancestors added a fresh dimension. These predecessors had at one time occupied many prominent castles and estates and it seemed logical at this stage of the search to see what had survived the centuries and which houses were still inhabited.

In terms of the search, I suppose Clare Island Castle should have pride of place. The stronghold of Granuaile, it is now little more than four walls, yet creates an impressive sight as the boat nears the island off the Atlantic coast, not far from Westport in county Mayo.

The Burkes of Castlehacket of whom the family of Ower is descended, derived from a common ancestor with the noble houses of Clanricarde and Mayo, and were seated on their estates of Castle Hacket and Annakeen, Co. Galway, from a very early period until driven out by Cromwell.[67]

Castle Hackett is situated close to Headford in co. Galway. An early eighteenth century building, it was partially burnt and rebuilt in the 1920s. Many years ago I recall calling unannounced, simply because I was on my way to Westport and had time to spare. I drove into the courtyard of a hugely impressive castle in what appeared to be excellent condition. There was no one around but I noticed a large side door open and ventured inside. I was in a long hall with many paintings on the walls. At the far end was a blazing fire and sitting in front in an easy chair was an old man with a blanket around him. I considered it unusual, to say the least, to finding myself sitting with him, hearing his life story and discussing the castle's history. He seemed less concerned with security than the thought that I was here to claim an interest in the property! He was Percy Paley, grandson of the Kirwans who had bought the estate from the Burkes about three hundred years previously. Shortly after our meeting Percy Paley died and I learned he had an extensive genealogical library which was auctioned off. I was unable to trace the buyer and often wonder if it contained the answer to the link between the Burkes of Becan and those of Ower and Castlehacket.

Menlough Castle in co. Galway, home of the Blakes, burnt to the ground in 1910. In it perished Eleanor, daughter of the 14th Baronet. It was Walter, the 10th Baronet. who married Barbara Burke of the Ower branch, both appearing on Father Tom's Blake-Burke tree.

A member of the Kirwan family built Cregg Castle in 1648. Situated at Corrandulla, Co. Galway, it is said to be the last fortified dwelling to be built west of the Shannon. It became the home of Richard Kirwan, the famous scientist, and the remains of his laboratory are still to be seen in the garden.[68] Richard was a cousin of my great, great, great grandmother, Mary Kirwan.

In Kilkenny, the twelfth century castle, remodelled in Victorian times, was the principal seat of the Butler family. James Butler, the 3rd Earl of Ormonde and Lord Justice of Ireland, purchased the Castle in 1391 and it remained in the family right up to 1935. The Earl was my eighteenth great grandfather, and his descendant Elizabeth, daughter of Walter, the 11th Earl, married Richard Burke, Lord Clanricarde. It was their daughter who married into the Bermingham family.

Charles Cavendish, son of the 9th Duke of Devonshire, resided at Lismore Castle and married Adele Astaire, sister of Fred. In recent years Fred Astaire was a frequent visitor to Lismore, as were many other Hollywood stars.[69] The computer programme was able to show that Charles Cavendish and I were direct descendants of the aforementioned Walter Butler and were in fact eleventh cousins.

Which brings me to Barretstown Castle (Fig.16). In the sixteenth century Joan Butler, granddaughter of the 8th Earl of Ormonde, married Rowland Eustace.[70] and moved into the Eustace family home at Barretstown, near Ballymore Eustace in county Kildare. It was not difficult to imagine the opulence of the Eustace dynasty whose territories included most of the eastern half of the country and who ranked second only to the Earls of Kildare as landowners. The contrast between the occupants of the castle in the 16th century and those of today could not be starker.

I approached Barretstown Castle as merely one on a list of houses to be inspected as part of my research, that is until I arrived and realised how it is used today. The history since the Eustace days is worth recalling.

The Borrowes family, descendants of the Norman de Burghs, acquired Barretstown as part of the Cromwellian settlements and resided there until 1924. Since then it has been owned by the cosmetics giant Elizabeth Arden and subsequently Galen Weston, who donated it to the Irish nation in 1977. In the early 1990s it came to the attention of Hollywood actor Paul Newman and in 1997 the Irish Government presented the Barretstown estate to Newman's "Hole In The Wall Gang Camp", designed to help children suffering from cancer and other serious illnesses.

The Barretstown charity runs a programme for youngsters that is recognised by the medical world as important in the recovery of these sick children. In the castle grounds they take part in a range of activities, which enable them to regain their self-esteem, find new skills, and talents, all of which help in dealing with their illnesses. I found it deeply affecting when shown around and one could hardly imagine a more worthwhile use for what was once the home of my ancestors. Donating my share of the proceeds from sales of this book to the Barretstown Fund seemed a most appropriate way to get value from the years of research.

[23]
A Distressing End

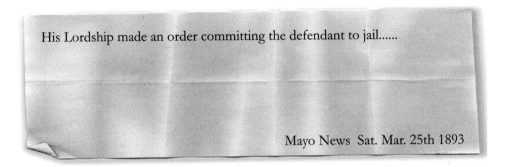

His Lordship made an order committing the defendant to jail......

Mayo News Sat. Mar. 25th 1893

John Francis Burke of Becan, who became coroner for county Mayo, was probably another grandson of Frank Burke and Mary Kirwan and hence a nephew of James Dominick. Although I had made no progress in my search for the mysterious Walter, I did discover through newspaper reports more about the children of John Francis. Recognising the impoverishment of Burke references toward the end of the last century, I was gradually able to piece together details of what appeared to be an unhappy end to the Becan saga.

The coroner had three sons, as we already knew. One was Dr. John Patrick of Claremorris who died in 1891 and who presumably left no children due to his death not long after his marriage. His brother Charles was living around the turn of the century in Becan with his two sisters. I felt that none of these married as no mention was made of children, nor did I uncover any records of such. The third son of John Francis, James, who was Clerk of the Claremorris Union[40] for many years, was also unmarried. Systematic searching of local newspapers revealed a most unfortunate end to his life.

The trouble started in February 1892 when James was accused of having lost deeds that had been deposited with him as Clerk of the Union. Further reference to this incident appeared in the Connaught Telegraph in April of the same year. Worse was to follow. In July, James was publicly criticised by the Board for exceeding his authority and paying an assistant to do his work. Bearing in mind that he had been Clerk since 1874, this must have been acutely embarrassing, to say the least.

Further trouble arose in the following year when James appeared before the Mayo Assizes in regard to debts and was sentenced to jail for six weeks with a stay of execution.

The impact of this on James must have been shattering. Shortly after, he was again publicly admonished, told to keep in his place and not to be dictating to the Board. This was in April 1893. He died within weeks on the 19th of July. As far as I could ascertain, no death notice appeared in any of the newspapers. Subsequently the Board of Guardians had to approve payment of funeral expenses, as the family was unable to do so.

Years later the following report appeared in the Connaught Telegraph dated Saturday, February the 19th 1898.

The Evicted Farm at Bekan

At the Ballyhaunis Petty Sessions on Monday, before Mr. Browne RM (in the Chair) and Dr. Creane JP, four summons for wilful trespass were brought at the suit of Lord Dillon against Ellen Burke, daughter of Mrs Burke, who was evicted from her farm at Bekan some time ago. The trespass is stated to have taken place on the evicted farm. In consequence of former litigation between Lord Dillon and the Burke family, the case excited much public interest.
Mr J.P. Mannion appeared for Lord Dillon and Mr T.D. Leech defended. Mr. Leech said the summons were only served on Friday last about 6 o'clock. The defendant's mother, who is a very old woman, considerably over 80 years of age, has been ill for some time. Some four or five years ago Lord Dillon issued a writ against these parties. For a considerable time the execution of the writ was stayed. He was however reluctantly compelled to serve the writ. The woman's son took forcible possession of the place. Lord Dillon was forced to take proceedings and the defendant's brother was tried and convicted at Castlebar Assizes and sentenced to 6 month's imprisonment. The defendant was fined 2s 6d in the first case of trespass and a fine of 10s was imposed in each of the other cases.

At first I believed it was another family of the same name, until it was pointed out to me that the defending counsel was unlikely to have represented other than a 'respectable' family. The County Coroner, John Francis Burke was born about 1809, which would have been close to the birth date of "Mrs Burke". She might have been a sister-in-law of John Francis who was given some farmland nearby and fell on hard times. The daughter Ellen was probably unmarried which would have explained the Burke name and the fact that it was her brother who was illegally involved previously. However, one way or another, the unfortunate circumstances preceding the death of James T. Burke, clerk of the Claremorris Union, were in marked contrast to those of his ancestors about whom songs were written and who married into the aristocracy of their generation. It was a distressing end to my research into those Burkes who remained in Becan and whom James Dominick left behind when he emigrated to seek his fortune in 1798.

[24]
Epilogue

So where do I go from here? What have I achieved? For one thing, I have found, and left a record of, events that occurred many years ago that will not now be forgotten.[72] I have to go on, if only to add to this record, to provide a sort of immortality for those people, who lived real lives, just as absorbing and personal as those of today. This sounds pompous and patronising, until one realises that these were real people, not just entries on a computer record.

I cannot provide all the intimate details of their lives, but at least I can imagine and speculate that their thoughts and feelings were no less interesting just because they lived in centuries past. Whether or not this is important is for others to judge. Whilst doubting if Annie Goodwin could ever have realised the significance of the letter to her son, I have finally come to understand it's importance, and why my subsequent research is of some value.

Annie set off for America with her new husband in 1888. Some time after writing the first letter accounting her husband's family history, she wrote two more letters which survived. The first gave a description of the circumstances of her youth.

My father died when I was only five years old and I can well remember going with my mother to visit his grave in St. John's Churchyard in Hackney, London and how I cried with her to think I should never see him again. My mother was a very young widow, very handsome and won the hearts of all who knew her. My two little brothers were placed in a good school by friends of my father, and I was left as a companion for my mother. We lived near my father's father who I remember well as being such a tall handsome man. He had four daughters living with him, all old maids, and I well remember as a child how I dreaded going to visit them, they were so strict and particular. I was very fond of school and used to go to Dalston to an excellent school and soon made great progress there. I was especially good at needlework and won money for making a perfect shirt measuring only six inches when I was only seven years old.

About this time there was another friend who appeared amongst us and soon persuaded my mother to change her sombre garment for more brightness and eventually persuaded her to change her name. Nature had certainly been lavish in her gifts upon him. He was tall, handsome and clever, with a splendid memory and seldom forgetting anything, and many envied my mother, although my father's people shut their doors and hearts against her for marrying again. All went smooth for some time and he was kindness itself to us but when the Crimea war broke out he decided to go and joined as an officer leaving us once more alone.

My grandmother, my mother's mother, died about this time and mother went to keep house for her father in Warwickshire. Oh! How I loved him he was so noble and good. I was placed in a boarding school and he used to come and see me every Sunday. About two weeks after Easter he said he was going to take me home to mother. Oh! What a glorious morning it was. We had to cross several fields, the sun was shining, birds were singing and the flowers looked so beautiful I could never forget it. He told me mother had a surprise for me, and so she had, for I found two little twin sisters awaiting me. Could anything be nicer - I had so longed for a sister and now thought my happiness complete. But how often when we poor mortals think our happiness complete it is only the commencement of trouble and so it proved for me, for shortly afterwards I was taken from school unfortunately for myself never to return.

I had to assist in nursing the little twins Mary and Martha. Mary grew so fast and was so attractable and loving we were soon inseparable and when eighteen months old she could talk quite plainly and used to carry her little sister who was very delicate and naturally a great pet. About this time we all had measles and then whooping cough and when poor little Mary was two years old she was seized with inflammation of the lung and died quite suddenly and then I thought no one had ever had such grief as mine. My grandfather, who was equally attached to our darling would insist on buying beautiful mourning for us all and said he never thought one little one could leave such a blank in a house. I am afraid we grieved too much for the pet little dreaming what great grief was in store for us all.

We were then living in Birmingham, England, and he was superintending the building, which was very high. He complained to one of the men of not feeling very well and said he would go down and did not know the men had just untied the ladder and the moment his weight touched the ladder he was dashed to the ground and killed instantly. Pen can never describe our grief and sorrow. He was loved by everyone, but by none so much as myself. I might truly say he taught me all that was truthful and noble in my character and above all things the secret of obtaining my own happiness in striving to make others happy, and to be content in whatever position I might be placed, and in all my sorrows, troubles and disappointment I never forgot his kind words of advice. I was eleven years old when he died, dear sister, and when I think of all the troubles I passed through from then until I was eighteen I would rather leave it as a dream untold, for so few would believe that one so young could have passed through safely. I will now begin again where some of the happier days of my life were spent...

The following pages are missing and so we can only speculate on the events of Annie's happier days. Annie painted a remarkable picture of her childhood. The eventual few years of marriage and her voyage home from Antigua with her four young children regrettably meant that the problems she writes about were relatively minor compared with what was to follow. She married my great grandfather at the age of twenty, so we know nothing about her troubles between the ages of eleven and eighteen. Unfortunately the remainder of the letter is missing. Her mother's re-marriage meant a move to Ireland (Colonel Brennan was from a Kilkenny family) and a new residence at 'The Grange' in Ballyfermot.

Annie's second letter described her arrival in America with her second husband, Colonel Murphy.

We arrived in New York, America, on Christmas Eve, 1888. On Christmas Day we went to Chapel and had our dinner at one of the largest halls in America. Thousands dine there every day. We had a beautiful dinner and thoroughly enjoyed it after the voyage. I shall never forget how curious it looked to see so many people enjoying their dinner. We were staying at a very nice hotel. On Christmas Day we went to Chapel. It made me feel quite at home. It was a lovely Chapel. The first place I went to visit was Castle Gardens. I was anxious to see where the poor emigrants landed. We went to Newark in a small but beautifully fitted up steamer. There was every accommodation, people even taking their horse and carriage on board. It is wonderful how many avail themselves of these steamers. They are very convenient for business people.
We went next to Philadelphia and spent some time there. It is a beautiful city so quiet and clean - it is spoken of as the dear old Quaker City. They have some beautiful buildings, some of them with beautiful marble frontages in black and white and some like concrete. We next went to Indianapolis and settled there. It is a beautiful city, and can boast of several beautiful parks...

Amongst my father's papers was a set of old sepia photographs, taken towards the end of the nineteenth century. As children we had seen them many times, although my father was unaware of their origin. They were of what appeared to be a mining town named Platteville, somewhere in the United States. The photographs suggested the town had been built around the mine. Recently, when clearing the contents of our attic on moving house, the photographs re-emerged and on examining them more closely, I noticed that one, taken in 1891, seemed to be of a local school in the state of Wisconsin. This reminded me of two photographs we had of Annie Goodwin on holiday, undated, which we learned from scratched markings on the back were taken in Wisconsin.

I examined the set of Platteville pictures more carefully and with the aid of a magnifying glass was amazed to find handwriting in pencil identifying the offices of 'J. W. Murphy' in one picture, and another inscribed 'the railway depot from which Annie left'. Clearly Platteville in Wisconsin was where Annie Goodwin visited in the later part of the nineteenth century and almost certainly was the home of her second husband. My father must have been given the photographs but it never occurred to him that they were part of his family history.

Someday I will get around to contacting Platteville. These anecdotes were constant reminders of what my vast collection of records, newspaper cuttings, family memorabilia, documents and other papers might contain.

The search goes on, and many questions continue to bother me to the present day. Some of the answers may even be buried in my own records. Who was Thomas Burke of Becan, who made a will in 1757 and from which of the leading Burke branches did he and the subsequent Becan Burkes emerge? Will we ever find a record of the marriage of James Dominick and Louisa Jane Collingwood? Where is James Dominick buried? Why did Louisa Jane move to Wexford with her third husband? What circumstances led to Father Tom being born a Catholic? Will a descendant of the Becan Burkes see this record and contact me? Or will it be a Hamilton Burke, or a Bermingham or a Kirwan? My interest has not waned and I have little doubt but that it will remain for as long as I can manage to make it up the steps of the National Library.

I continue to be fascinated by the fact that so much has been discovered by chance – an old envelope lying among my father's photographs, Michael's discovery of his distant cousin in Ireland, the record of a Burke-Kirwan wedding in an eighteenth century newspaper.

Having exercised an enormous amount of care and attention, the Royal College of Surgeons eventually completed the copying of James Dominick's Journal, and presented bound copies to the family. The original is now in the Archives of the Mercer Library, valued not just for its medical content, but also because in their view any document written two hundred years ago is of historical value and should be preserved. It has a covering insert, which reads:

James Dominick Burke 1780-1822
Of Becan, Co. Mayo

Attended RCSI 1788/89

Passed as Navy Surgeon 3rd Rate
RCS London, 15th May 1800

Married Louisa Jane Collingwood
Of the Distinguished English Naval Family

Appointed Surgeon at Pembroke Dockyard
30th November 1815

Died June 1822 Survived by his Widow and Six Children

We had come a long way since my father first showed me the letter from Annie Goodwin to her son. I still find it disconcerting to think that had she not written it, this account of a family history would not exist.

References

1. Mr Hugh D W Lees (died aged 75 in 1982) was a genealogist and local historian. He spent over 25 years compiling an indexed survey of the inhabitants of over 60 of Lowestoft's oldest streets. He was president of both the Suffolk Genealogy Society (now the Suffolk Family History Society - SFHS) and the Old Lowestoft and District Society. He was also an honorary member of the Lowestoft Archaeological and Local History Society. These items were bequeathed to the SFHS upon his decease. Hugh Lees' collection is ref. 'Acc 1113 - Hugh Lees Survey of Lowestoft 1784 - 1974, held at the Lowestoft Record Office. www.suffolkcc.gov.uk/sro/ (Information courtesy of Louise Clarke, Lowestoft Record Office).

2. Now part of the UK National Archives.(www.nationalarchives.gov .uk). Not to be confused with the Public Record office of Ireland.

3. UK National Archives: PRO, Kew: ADM section, various references.

4. UK National Archives: PRO, Kew: 15th Hussars; various records.

5. 'Pedigree of the Clanricardes and also of the Burkes of Ower through eleven hundred years' by Oliver J. Burke, Barrister-at-Law, 2 March 1866.

6. The Royal College of Surgeons in Ireland (RCSI) was founded in1784. It holds records created by the Royal College of Surgeons since 1784 and records of other institutions including Mercer's Hospital, Meath Hospital, Surgical Society of Ireland along with records created by various individuals. It is located in Mercer Street Lower, Dublin 2. (www.rcsi.ie)

7. Wexford Family History Society, 24 Partlands, Wexford, Co. Wexford, Ireland.

8. The National Library of Ireland was established in 1877 when the State bought a substantial portion of the library of the Royal Dublin Society. Since its foundation it has endeavoured to collect and preserve all material of Irish interest. It is the legal deposit library for all works published in Ireland. It is located at Kildare Street, Dublin 2. (www.nli.ie)

9. The Registry of Deeds was established in Ireland in 1708 to record land transactions, including ownership, tenure and leases. Indexes to grantors and places are available for the research of these records. It is located at Henrietta Place Dublin 1. (www.irlgov.ie/landreg/)

10. Royal Irish Academy, the academy for the sciences and humanities for the whole of Ireland. It has an extensive library of books and manuscripts. It is located at 19 Dawson Street, Dublin 2. (www.ria.ie)

11. National Archives of Ireland, the major repository for material generated by government and state funded bodies. Formerly the Public Record (founded in 1867) it was amalgamated with the State Paper Office in 1988. Its major holdings include the 1901 and 1911 census returns for the 32 counties of Ireland and surviving Wills and Administrations. It is located at Bishop Street, Dublin 8. (www.nationalarchives.ie)

12. The Representative Church Body Library, commonly known as the RCB Library is the Church of Ireland's principal repository for its manuscripts and documents. It contains records from parishes, dioceses and non-current records of church administration. The manuscript collection includes papers of prominent clergy, laity and Church of Ireland organisations and societies. The library is located at Braemor Park, Churchtown, Dublin 14. (www.library.ireland.anglican.org)

13. 'Memorials of the Dead, Counties Wicklow and Wexford' by Brian Cantwell. These volumes were privately printed and donated to the major national libraries and to local libraries in the two counties.

14. The 'Journal of the Association for the Preservation of the Memorials of the Dead in Ireland' was published between 1880 and 1920. It was continued as the 'Journal of Irish Memorials Association' from 1921 to 1931.

15. National Library of Wales holds a large collection of genealogical material including civil registration indexes, census returns, parish records and probate records from local Welsh courts. It is located in Aberystwyth, Ceredigion. (www.llgc.org.uk)

16. Society of Genealogists has the largest collection of copies of parish registers in the UK. It is located at 14 Charterhouse Buildings, Goswell Road, London, EC1M 7BA. (www.sog.org.uk)

17. The logs and lists of appointments were copied from papers of Brigadier

W.A.C. Collingwood which are in possession of a branch of the Collingwood family in the UK along with family histories and one-name studies

18. 'Nelson – A Personal History' by Christopher Hibbert, Viking Press 1994.

19. Naval 'Commanders'. UK National Archives (formerly PRO): Kew.

20. 'The Topographical Dictionary of Ireland' by Samuel Lewis, Published London 1837. Provides a history and statistics for all civil parishes, market towns and post towns in the 32 counties of Ireland. Some counties have been reprinted as separate publications.

21. Registers of Marriages – July 1828, Parish of St. George, Hanover Square. Fol.198 No.515.

22. The London Court case was reported in a number of newspapers, but principally the London Times as stated. The Dublin Evening Packet and Morning Post also carried reports.

23. The Stephen Street information came from the Index to Original Wills of the Diocese of Dublin 1800-1858 page 105 – Gilbert Library.

24. Walkers Hibernian Magazine: 1804 p.763, Marriages December 1804: 'On Summer-hill, Cufack Rooney Efq. of Arran-quay, to mifs Charlotte Mullay, daughter of the late James Mullay, Esq., of Gloucefter-ftreet'.

25. Burial records of the Northern Cemetery, Dunedin, New Zealand: No.3528 Lot 3a Block 112.

26. Otago Daily Times – 19/09/1933.

27. 'Old Kerry Records' by Agnes Hickson, 2nd series, Watson & Hazell, London 1874.

28. The 'Index to Wills and Administrations' are available on open shelf in the National Archives of Ireland, Bishop Street, Dublin 8.

29. Burke's 'Genealogical and Heraldic Dictionary of the Landed Gentry of Ireland', 1912 edition.

30. Bekan is a civil parish and Bekan House is located in the village. Note that the spelling of Bekan varies according to source i.e. Bacon, Beacon and Becan are also found. The village is spelt Bekan on current maps.

31. 'Beacan/Bekan – Portrait of an East Mayo Parish', edited by Fr. Michael O'Comer and Nollaig O'Muraile, published 1986 by Fr. Michael Comer, The Presbytery, Ballinrobe, Co. Mayo.

32. A census of the population was taken every 10 years from 1821. The 1901 and 1911 census returns are the only surviving returns for all 32 counties which are open for research. While no census returns survive for 1861-1891, some do survive covering some parts of the country for 1821-1851. Census material is held at the National Archives of Ireland, Dublin.

33. The Spinning Wheel List or the Flax Growers Bounty List 1796. A list of names of the persons to whom the Irish Linen Board awarded spinning wheels in return for planting specific acreages of flax. It is available in the National Library of Ireland (ref Ir.677 L3) and has also been published on CD .

34. 'Statistical Survey of the County of Mayo' by James McPartlan M.D., published Dublin 1801.

35. A planxty is an Irish melody for the harp.

36. On page 88 of the Bekan book (see endnote 31) is 'An Irish Song from Bekan' c.1760, translated by Nollaig O Muraile

37. 'Index to the Prerogative Wills of Ireland 1536-1810' by Sir Arthur Vicars. Published Dublin 1897 and reprinted by the Genealogical Publishing Co. Baltimore (1969) and (1997).

38. The Irish Public Record Office was destroyed by fire in 1922. The Will collection was lost, although some indexes did survive. These include the 'Index to the Prerogative Wills of Ireland 1536-1810'. (See 37 above).

39. The reference to HM Cressy was in my father's papers but no source is available.

40. The Boards of Guardians were established under the Poor Law Act, 1838. The Act divided the country into a number of Poor Law Unions, each of which had a board of Guardians and a workhouse. The members of the Board of Guardians were usually local landowners who were responsible for the social welfare and public health of the people within the Poor Law Union.

41. Marriage certificate: District of Birmingham, County of Warwickshire, No.83, St. Peters Church 1884.

42. These papers are in a private collection.

43. Connaught Telegraph: articles by 'Antiquarian' published on the 26/6/1937 and 21/8/1937.

44. 'Houses of Kerry' by Valerie Bary, Ballinakella Press 1994.

45. Registry of Deeds: Mayo Land Index 1739-1810 book 39, vol.427, page 204, no.270576.

46. Registry of Deeds: 1834, vol.22, no.35.

47. 'The Story of the Drumboe Martyrs', printed by McKinney & O'Callaghan, Main Street, Letterkenny, Co. Donegal (no date).

48. 'No Other Law – The Story of Liam Lynch and the Irish Republic' by Florence O'Donoghue, Irish Press Ltd. 1954.

49. 'West Brit', a term used in Ireland for persons holding pro-British views.

50. Registry of Deeds: vol.759; page 302; no.515637.

51. Registry of Deeds: vol.440; page 223; no.204143.

52. Registry of Deeds: vol.8; page 236.

53. The 'Tribes of Galway' are the fourteen families who dominated the political, commercial and social life of Galway City from the 1400s to the 1700s. The families were; Athy, Blake, Bodkin, Browne, D'Arcy, Deane, ffont, ffrench, Joyce, Kirwan, Lynch, Martin, Morris and Skerritt.

54. 'Genealogy from Milesius' by Douglas Agar Kirwan and John Water Kirwan. Royal Irish Academy, shelf no. RR64D.27

55. Genealogical Office, Dublin. Ref: GO. Mss. 9854/5/6 Kirwan.

56. Irish Press 1st June 1951 M.J.McM.

57. Genealogical Office, Dublin. Ref: GO.Ms.9856.

58. Registry of Deeds: vol.288 page 215 no.188688.

59. The Gilbert Library forms a cornerstone of the Dublin City Library and Archive and is comprised of books and manuscripts collected by the archivist and historian Sir. John T. Gilbert. Dublin City Library and Archive is located at 138-144 Pearse Street, Dublin 2. (www.iol.ie/dublincitylibrary)

60. 'All Souls' by Michael Coady, The Gallery Press 1997.

61. Genealogical Office, Dublin. Ref: GO.Ms.9856.

62. Genealogical Office, Dublin. Ref: GO.Ms.4183.

63. Burkes 'Extinct and Dormant Peerages'. Pub. 1883, London.

64. 'The Complete Peerage' by G.E.C edited by Hon. Vicary Gibbs (1910).

65. Connaught Telegraph, 28th April 1894.

66. 'History of Mayo' (5 Volumes) by J.F. Quinn. Published by Brendan Quinn, Ballina, Mayo, Ireland 1993.

67. Genealogical Office, Dublin. Ref: GO.Ms.112.

68. 'A Guide to Irish Country Houses' by Mark Bence-Jones, Constable, London 1988.

69. 'At Home in Ireland' by Ava Astaire McKenzie, Roberts Rinehart Publishers 1988.

70. Burkes Peerage: various editions.

71. Griffith's Valuation. A listing of occupiers of land and properties in Ireland compiled for land tax purposes. It was begun in 1846 and is widely available on microfiche in Irish libraries, and also available for purchase on CD.

72. The author's family database can be accessed on the Flyleaf Press website at www.flyleaf.ie/burkedatabase.htm. This provides access to all of the author's data, excluding living persons. Full instructions on the database are also provided on this page. See also the Preface for further details on this source.

Sources

The research required a wide range of background information on events, places and families, some of which are specifically cited in the reference section. The major books and archival sources used by the author for this purpose are listed below.

Libraries and Archives

Genealogical Office, Dublin:

F.S. Burke Collection
Unregistered pedigree index
McAnlis consolidated index
Teeling papers
Longfield maps
Reports on Private Collections
Collectanea Genealogical

National Archives of Ireland:

Topographical Dictionary of Ireland by Samuel Lewis, 1837
Vicars Index to Prerogative Wills of Ireland 1536 – 1810, published 1897
The Dublin Almanac and General Register of Ireland 1835, 1845 and 1855
Griffiths Primary Valuations
Tithe Applotment Books
Irish Census Returns, 1901 and 1911
Index to Diocesan Tuam Wills 1648 – 1858
Wills and Administrations
Marriage Licences Bonds

National Library of Ireland:

Newspapers:

Connaught Telegraph
Connaught Journal
Dublin Evening Mail
Dublin Evening Packet
Irish Press
Mayo Constitution
The Times (London)
Tuam Herald
Western Chronicle

Wexford Conservative

Publications:

Annals of the Four Masters
Burkes Landed Gentry
Burkes Landed Gentry of Ireland
Burkes Irish Family Records
Burkes Extinct and Dormant Peerages
Burkes Peerage and Baronetage
Commoners of Great Britain and Ireland
The Complete Peerage by G.E.C edited by Hon. Vicary Gibbs, 1910
Dictionary of National Biography, Oxford University Press 1973
Hayes 'Manuscript Sources for the History of Irish Civilisation'
O'Harts Irish Pedigrees
O'Kief Coshe Mang Slieve Lougher & Upper Blackwater in Ireland

Directories:

The Gentleman's and Citizen's Almanac
Leet's Directory of Market Towns
Pettigrew & Oulton 1835
Pigot's Commercial Directory of Ireland
Slater's Commercial Directory of Ireland
Thom's Directory 1865
Watson's Almanac 1830
Walker's Hibernian Magazine
Wilson's Dublin Directory

Microfilm:
   Parish registers
   Abstracts of Tuam Wills

Representative Church Body Library, Dublin:

Convert Rolls
Bagwell: Ireland under the Tudors

Royal Irish Academy, Dublin:

Books of Survey and Distribution 1650 – 1690
Strafford's Survey Book of Co. Mayo 1635 – 1637
Hardiman's History of Galway
Kirwin Pedigree
Local genealogical and historical society journals

Gilbert Library, Dublin:

Freeman's Journal
Index to Public Wills 1800 – 1858

Public Record Office, Kew, London:

Admiralty Records:
   Captain's logs
   Muster Lists
   Master's Logs
   Bounty papers
   Surgeons

British Museum:

Lansdowne Manuscripts
Harleian Collection

National Maritime Museum, Greenwich:

Admiral Collingwood memorabilia
Painting 'Death of Nelson' by Devis

Public Record Office of Northern Ireland.
Royal College of Physicians of Ireland.
Registry of Deeds, Dublin.
Public Libraries in Ireland.

Bibliography

Books:
  Bary, Valerie, Houses of Kerry, Ballinakella Press, Whitegate, Co. Clare 1994.
  Baynham, Henry, From the Lower Deck - the Old Navy 1780-1840,
    Hutchinson & Co., 1969.
  Belden, K.D., The Story of the Westminster Theatre, 1965
  Bourke, Eamonn, Burke - People and Places, 4th Edition 2001.
  Brady's Records of Cork, Cloyne and Ross, 1863
  Chambers, Anne, Chieftain to Knight, Wolfhound Press 1983.
  Coady, Michael, All Souls', The Gallery Press 1997.
  Cyclopedia of New Zealand, The, 1905
  Grenham, John, Tracing Your Irish Ancestors, Gill and Macmillan, 2nd Edition
    1992.
  Hibbert, Christopher, Nelson - A Personal History, Viking Press, 1994
  Hickson, Mary Agnes, Old Kerry Records, Watson & Hazell, 1872
  King, Jeremiah, County Kerry Past and Present, Mercier Press, 1931
  Lyons, J.B., The Irresistible Rise of the R.C.S.I.
  McKinney & O'Callaghan, The Story of the Drumboe Martyrs, Letterkenny.
  Mankenzie, E., The Life of Lord Collingwood, W & T Fordyce, 1841
  Marquess of Sligo, Westport House and the Brownes, 1992.
  Anson's Voyage Round The World, Everyman's Library, edited by Ernest Rhys,
    J.M. Dent & Son Ltd., London 1911
  Naval Commanders, published c.1826
  O'Brien, Maureen, The Burke/Bourke Clan
  O'Connor, Mary, When Battle's Done, The Kerryman Ltd., Tralee, 1996
  O'Donoghue, Florence, No Other Law – The story of Liam Lynch and the Irish
    Republic, Irish Press Ltd., 1954.
  Ryan, James, Irish Records: Sources for Family and Local History, Flyleaf Press
    1997.
  Quinn, J.F., History of Mayo, Mayo 1993.
  Who's Who in New Zealand, 3rd edition, 1932

Computer Software

Steed, John, "Brother's Keeper", Version 6.0 for Windows, 1997

Appendix:

Annie's Letter

"In Frank's last letter he told me he had received a Staff Appointment in County Carlow. He expects to be there so long as he is in the Army. I am very glad - I was afraid he would have to go to India and it is anything but pleasant travelling around with little folk. They were to start for Ireland on the 2nd November - it will be a nice little trip for them all to visit each other - it is only about 35 miles from Carlow to Dublin.

"Oh how gladly I will answer your questions my dear son about your dear father although I have not been very prompt in doing so please forgive the delay.

"Your father was born in ? England on the 13th of December 1815. His father was a surgeon in the Navy. His name was James Dominic Burke. His mother was a niece of Admiral Collingwood - named Louisa Collingwood. Your father had four sisters and one brother Russell. Your grandfather Burke died at the age of forty two leaving six children. Your father often told me about your grandmother marrying a second time to an officer in the English Army. He was very kind and they got along nicely until one day a favourite horse belonging to the family got sick and the doctor said it must be shot and when the step-father shot it your father and his brother were so indignant they determined to run away and enlist and when their friends found them they would not be bought out of the Army they enlisted in an Infantry Regiment. Your father's love of horses soon made him anxious to join a Cavalry Regiment and through the influence of your grandmother got transferred to the 15th Hussars and remained with the 15th until he obtained the Staff Appointment in Aldershot in 1860 where I met him. Your Uncle Russell remained with his regiment until he died. He died in Chatham - he was an Army Apothecary at the time of his death and your Aunt got a good pension. He was dead before I met your

father. Two of your father's sisters died unmarried - one married a solicitor and died leaving a young family and Maria, the eldest one, promised her dying sister to never leave her children and so faithfully kept her word, she never married but remained with them and even went to Otago, New Zealand, with them. I received many letters from her while your father was living but none after his death.

"Your grandmother Burke married three times and was a widow when she died. Your father had been away fifteen years when he was coming to Aldershot and hoped to spend a few years with his mother but poor fellow was to be disappointed - she died quite suddenly when eating her breakfast one morning when he was on his way home. Your aunt Maria had not started for New Zealand then and your father and Uncle Russell gave up all claim on everything and gave all to her. She turned everything to money and, of course, took it with her. Your father had a cousin in London, a retired paymaster of the Navy, named Walter Burke. They had a splendid home. I received a warm welcome from him and his wife and daughters when we went to London when we first married. He had one daughter a nun - the other three were very nice girls. He has been dead for some years. Do you remember old Lady Gavagan - she was a cousin of your fathers - sister to Mrs. Burke. Her son is a Colonel in the Army. You remember him I think - he was Major Gavagan when we were in Aldershot - you remember playing with his son Frank.

"Then another cousin of your fathers, Bernard Burke, he was, strange to say, a young officer in the Crimean War and slept in the same tent with Col. Brennan. He is now stationed in Dublin as Major Burke, Paymaster of Pensions. He was a very nice gentleman and often visited me in Aldershot and used to say he little thought when in the Crimea that a cousin of his would marry into Col. Brennan's family. These are all the friends I have met on your father's side. I hope you will be able to make out my rambling account. I will give you an account of my family circle in my next. I am afraid if I write much more in this you will never have patience to wade through. I know you will be glad to know myself and Mr. Murphy are quite well and although we are not making a fortune we have, thank God, been able to hold our own during this troublesome year. I am glad to say everything is quietened down now and business improving every day.

"I can scarcely believe it is so near Xmas. I believe this letter will scarcely arrive in time to wish you and dear Father Walshe a happy Xmas. Oh what I would give to be with you on that day - thank God I can at least be with you at the holy feast for isn't it the same all over the world and I can be with you in spirit - do not forget me but say one little prayer for my intention.

Mr. Murphy joins in love to you and believe me

Your affectionate mother

Annie Murphy

Index

S

Saint Beacuan 82
Saunders, Rear-Admiral Sir George 56
Spotfield Estate 81, 127
Spotfield estate 141
Strongbow 134, 135
Suffolk 15, 161
Survey of Co. Mayo 82

T

Taylor, Hugh 37, 51, 52, 57
Treaty of Limerick 137
Tregunnan 30
Trinity College 32

U

U.S. Virgin Islands 21
Uncle Tom 7, 12, 25, 27, 86, 131
US Army 12

W

Wales 12, 25, 26, 39, 40, 56, 136, 163
Wallscourt, Baron 136
Wallscourt, Lord 136
Walshe, Annie 119, 121, 132, 134
Warwick 134
Weston, Galen 149
Westport 85, 86, 88, 89, 112, 113, 137,
    138, 147, 170
West Indies 12, 18, 20
Wexford 5, 30, 32, 33, 36, 42, 47, 48, 49,
    57, 58, 59, 60, 61, 73, 74, 79, 80,
    92, 93, 95, 158, 162, 163
Wexford Burkes 80
William de Burgo 80, 143, 145
William the Conqueror 27, 145
Woodville 112
World War I 14
Wouldham 36